# FLYING CARS

© 2005 by Éditions Favre SA, Lausanne, Switzerland

First published as *Les Voitures Volantes* by Éditions Favre SA in 2005
This edition published by Haynes Publishing in June 2011

A catalogue record for this book is available from the British Library.

ISBN 978 0 85733 091 8

Library of Congress control no. 2010943423

Published by Haynes Publishing,
Sparkford, Yeovil, Somerset BA22 7JJ, UK.
Tel: 01963 442030 Fax: 01963 440001
Int. tel: +44 1963 442030
Int. fax: +44 1963 440001
E-mail: sales@haynes.co.uk
Website: www.haynes.co.uk

Haynes North America Inc.,
861 Lawrence Drive, Newbury Park,
California 91320, USA.

Original design by Julien Notter and Sébastien Vigne
Translated and adapted by Jon Pressnell

Cover image: ConvAirCar 118,
San Diego Aerospace Museum

Printed in the USA by Odcombe Press LP,
1299 Bridgestone Parkway, La Vergne, TN 37086

# FLYING CARS

## The extraordinary history of cars designed for tomorrow's world

**Patrick J. Gyger**

with the collaboration of Francis Valery

# Contents

# Introduction: Elsewhere as the horizon

*"Once, the world was not as it has since become. Once it worked in a way different from the way it works now; its very flesh and bones, the physical laws that governed it, were ever so slightly different from the ones we know. It had a different history, too, from the history we know the world to have had, a history that implied a different future from the one that has actually come to be, our present."*

*John Crowley,* Love and Sleep

It seems in the nature of man to be forever extending his living space. In the beginning, the surface world was the only one to exist. To the two dimensions of this world-view a third was quickly added, that of verticality.

From simple personal travel to the bulk transport of people and goods, man has always wanted to go further and faster in his appropriation of the universe. The human thirst to journey other than on the land is in no way a natural necessity but springs from a purely cultural desire, ceaselessly fuelled by our imagination, not least through the boundless futurism of science-fiction. This is a two-way traffic, a permanent dialogue between the Real and the Imaginary. Scientists are inspired by the stimulating visions of artists, and these in turn base their anticipatory speculations on the technological climate of their time.

With the coming of the industrial era, people began to dream of vehicles that had multiple functions. Born out of science-fiction literature, the idea of a genuinely all-terrain vehicle capable of travelling on dry land and in and under the water, as well as being able to take to the air, was never, however, a realistic prospect. Technological impossibilities and a lack of practical interest from the public meant that such a vehicle would always remain a fantasy.

On the other hand, bi-functional vehicles – able to be used both on land and either on the surface of the water or in the sky – did become a reality. Not least for military purposes, people began to construct amphibious cars and hovercraft, the latter machines being essentially waterborne but capable of venturing onto terra firma. Alongside this, independent inventors, often American, battled to make a reality of the flying car or 'roadable airplane' – whether giving priority to the automotive or aeronautical element of the machine.

This book seeks to tell the story of these fascinating machines, whether as portrayed in the imagination of writers, illustrators and film-makers or as the concrete projects of hobbyists and eccentrics, men ingenious and burning with enthusiasm, whose destiny was often anything but banal.

Because if flying cars have been the subject of many a dream, they have also been built, sometimes even coming close to production. The subject matter is thus not the marginalia it might seem. Furthermore, examining the history of flying cars allow us to question how humanity uses the technologies at its disposal. It allows us a glimpse of those moments, exhilarating or exasperating, when fiction passes – or fails to pass – into reality.

In the air, on land, and even under the water! An illustration by H. Thiret for *L'avion sous-marin* by A. Teidor and F. Duthuit (Tallanier, no.204 in the collection Bibliothèque des Grandes Aventures, 1928).

The Autoplane of Glenn Curtiss on display
at the first Pan-American Aeronautic
Exposition of 8-15 February 1917.

**1.**

# Pioneering times

At the beginning of the 20th century the car and the plane, which were still recent inventions, grew up side-by-side, and followed similar lines of development. It wasn't long before thoughts turned to bringing them together in a single machine.

### An almost natural hybrid

On a technical level the common points between an aircraft and a car allowed early aviators to use automobile engines and parts without a second thought. In a social context, meanwhile, the idea gained ground that the man in the street would ultimately annex the air just as easily and rapidly as he had already colonised the roads: the transition to the third dimension would be just a question of time and means. A personal aeroplane would soon be as popular – and banal – as having one's own car. Marrying car and aircraft quickly became a dream shared by countless people, from weekend hobbyists to the most highly-qualified of engineers, taking in on the way industrial designers and those who had their own futurist visions, often inspired by science-fiction.

The principal value of such a dual-purpose vehicle is that it can liberate both the car and the aeroplane from their particular constraints. A road-going vehicle, which is rarely amphibious, is tied to the ground, and to roads on which it cannot exceed a speed restricted by the limits of technology and the norms of safety; an aeroplane, on the other hand, although it is capable of higher speeds and is – at least in appearance – 'as free as the air', remains to all intents and purposes dependent on aerodromes, and these are often far from town or city centres.

Furthermore, a single machine, capable of travel both on land and in the air, should in theory allow a considerable reduction in journey times, particular over middling distances. If taking a plane saves time, the need to get to the departure airport from home and then at the other end to travel from the airport to one's final destination, plus the inevitable delays in transit, often takes away the advantages of air travel.

So combining the possibilities of the two different machines in a hybrid vehicle seems an eminently logical step forward, a completely legitimate fantasy: taking the aero-car from the garage and making for the nearest straight stretch of tarmac from which one can take to the air in full glorious freedom...

But what sort of bastard machine is likely to emerge from this union of different technologies? The design brief is perfectly clear: that the vehicle should be cheap, durable, practical and simple. In other words it should be as easy to fly in the sky as to drive on the road. Unfortunately this is conceptually nigh-on impossible. A plane must be as light as possible while having a powerful engine; the ideal car, in contrast, should be above all sturdy and safe, spacious and comfortable – which means being relatively heavy – and should have moderate fuel consumption, which means no more than moderate power. If you start to get into the detail, it's evident that a certain standard of tyre will be indispensable for safe landings, as well as powerful dampers – not to mention a cabin that can resist stresses that have no equivalent in the use of a normal car on normal roads. Put another way, the development

M. John Progrès.

of the perfect aero-car is a technological challenge – a real squaring of the circle – that risks creating a means of transport that performs poorly both on the road and in the air.

### Early ventures

Chronicles tell that in 1772 the abbé Desforges, canon of the French town of Etampes, built a wheeled vehicle equipped with wings, described as a 'cabriolet'. His machine, incorporating weather-protection and moving wings operated by the pilot, was hauled to the top of a tower in the town, from which it was supposed to take flight. The good cleric got off lightly, with nothing more than the destruction of his machine and a sprained ankle.

In 1781 another Frenchman, Jean-Pierre Blanchard (who would a few years later make the first hot-air balloon flight on the North American

The personal flying vehicle was thought up before either the car or the plane became a reality. Here we see Mr John Progrès riding his airborne steam locomotive in a scene from *Le Monde tel qu'il sera* by Emile Souvestre (1846); illustration by O.Penguilly.

*At Saint-Pair the principal means of communication had been established, for greater convenience, in a space previously abandoned to the wind and to the birds. The streets were left almost exclusively to pedestrians. You could see flying-cabs, omnibus-balloons and winged tilburies passing each other in every direction: the ether, finally mastered, had become a new field of human activity.*

*Emile Souvestre, Le Monde tel qu'il sera
(1846, Michel Lévy frères).*

EAST RIVER BRIDGE. NEW YORK.

A post card from 1908: at the beginning of the 20th century people were already imagining making a car fly.

*The little aeropiles (as for no particular reason they were distinctively called) were of an altogether different type. Several of these were going to and fro in the air. They were designed to carry only one or two persons, and their manufacture and maintenance was so costly as to render them the monopoly of the richer sort of people. Their sails, which were brilliantly coloured, consisted only of two pairs of lateral air floats in the same plane, and of a screw behind. Their small size rendered a descent in any open space neither difficult nor disagreeable, and it was possible to attach pneumatic wheels or even the ordinary motors for terrestrial tragic to them, and so carry them to a convenient starting place.*

*H. G. Wells,* When the Sleeper Wakes

continent), built a 'flying ship' with four oval wings and a propeller that was supposed to be hand-operated. He wisely stayed on the ground.

Crossing the Channel and moving to a new century, in 1808 an English inventor, Sir George Cayley, drew up the Coachman's Carrier, a mixture of boat, glider and wheeled vehicle. Needless to say, it never took flight. No more did the Aerial Steam Carriage of William Samuel Henson, pompously named Ariel after the spirit of the air in Shakespeare's *The Tempest*. It was a sort of small coach with a long cruciform-shaped tail, topped by an immense wing like a flat fish, and equipped with a propeller driven by a steam engine. It was an ambitious venture, at least on paper: Frederick Marriott, the publicist for Henson's company, The Aerial Transit Company, made several drawings of the Ariel in flight – above the pyramids, in India, or over London, which evidently made an impression. But the project stayed at the pen-and-ink stage.

William Henson probably wasn't trying to build a machine that was at the same time capable of being used on the road as well as in the air; he was more likely trying simply to invent a viable form of aircraft.

The same can be said of Romanian Trajan Vuia and his aeroplane of 1905. With its structure mounted on four wheels and its steering by wheel it looked even more like a car. Indeed, it was tested near Paris for several weeks without its wings, perhaps making people think it was a new model of car. In March 1906 it managed to fly ten yards or so, at an altitude of three feet, and this first success was followed by several other flights, making Trajan Vuia one of the first people in the world to have flown a plane.

Three years later, whilst Igor Sikorsky was working on his helicopter, fellow Russian Vladimir Tatarinov began to build his Aeromobile, a car with four wire-spoked wheels and an enormous five-blade propeller at the front, the whole surmounted by a system of four six-blade rotors. The prop and the rotors were powered by a 25bhp water-cooled engine and the machine weighed more than a ton. But the army, which was financing the project, decided that the work was taking too long, and cut funding.

With the benefit of hindsight, many of these projects were surely influenced by the work of novelists such as Albert Robida, Jules Verne, André Laurie and their predecessors, and their creators seem often to have confused fiction and reality. Doubtless this was out of an over-developed sense of optimism, as if science and its application to technology had moved the limits of feasibility beyond the human horizon. Or did it suffice to draw one's dreams for them to take form and become part of real life?

Far more within the realms of reality was the presence at New York's Pan-American Aeronautic Exposition of 1917 of a hybrid machine conceived by Glenn Hammond Curtiss, the Autoplane Model 11 or

Aerial boats: an illustration for *Ignis*, a novel by Didier de Chousy that appeared in *La Science illustrée* no.449 (1896).

In 1981 the Romanian post office celebrated the 75th anniversary of the flight by Trajan Vuia, on 18 March 1906; Vuia was one of the first men to fly a powered machine, which in his case looked remarkably like a car with wings.

Another photograph, dated 13 February 1917, of the Curtiss Autoplane (also called the Autolandplane or Curtiss Model 11) during the first Pan-American Aeronautic Exposition.

Autolandplane. This was just 13 years after the first successful flight by the Wright brothers, on 17 December 1903, and nine years after the launch of the legendary Model T Ford.

This tri-plane with its 39ft (12m) wingspan was nicknamed the 'Flying Limousine' because the pilot/driver was seated at the front with the two passengers side by side at the rear of the cabin. A system of chains and gear-wheels transmitted the power from the engine of the car part – made in aluminium – to the single propeller at the rear of the cabin. The wings and the tail section were easily detachable, so the road-going element could be used as a normal car.

Glenn Curtiss was far from being a novice: the first American to officially hold a pilot's licence, in 1911, he was also the first person to design aeroplanes for general sale. Not only that, but his company produced more than 10,000 planes during the First World War. There is no doubt that Curtiss belongs in the pantheon of American aviation alongside the Wright brothers. In fact he had already invented a hybrid aircraft, a flying boat, a vehicle that had a bright future before it under the name hydraplane. Despite the experience of its creator, the Autoplane was nonetheless a failure: capable of making only short jumps, it was quickly abandoned.

The following year a certain Felix Longobardi applied with all due process for a five-page patent (the first of its type) concerning a 'Combination Vehicle' that looked as if had come straight from the pages of a science-fiction novel. The general appearance of the machine was like a fully-enclosed boat hull topped by a periscope and a cylindrical cabin with portholes. This was supported on two wheeled axles of which the front one was equipped with a pair of wings which could be folded upwards. Three horizontal propellers were mounted under the chassis, for vertical displacement, while a single front airscrew and two at the rear looked after horizontal travel. The machine was thus intended to be at the same time a boat, a submarine, a car and a plane.

Another project of a few years later was on similar lines. This was the 'Combined Automobile and Aeroplane' of Anton Jezek, patented in 1928 and looking like a flying motor-bus. Equipped with four enormous wheels, it had an impressively large engine at the front, driving the propeller. Curiously, the wings were minuscule and recalled the tail fins of a fish.

It goes without saying that the machines of Longobardi and Jezek never left the drawing board.

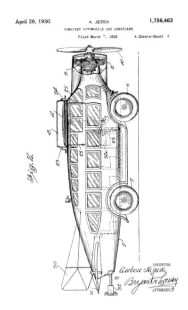

The 1928 patent application by Anton Jezek, for a 'Combined Automobile and Aeroplane'.

### The persistence of a vision

To appreciate the tenacity of the desire to take freely to the air from one's own home, all you need to do is dip into some real-world records, those of patent applications in the United States.

Here, year after year, you can find diagrams with lengthy descriptions of all those inventions over which their creators sought to protect their intellectual property. Whether or not the idea would ever see the light of day is of course another matter.

The number of flying cars is staggering: more than 80 since 1918. Evidently the great majority never flew and remained mere paper dreams. All the same, here is the proof that the fantasy of a road-going aircraft, forever elusive but kept alive by its portrayal in science-fiction, has for a century seemed on the cusp of becoming reality.

In their patent applications each new inventor announces that he is the first to give serious thought to the question and that he has introduced crucial technical innovations which will guarantee the success of his machine – forgetting, of course, all those equally fruitful and conclusive initiatives with which history in this domain is littered...

The Curtiss Model E amphibian, taking off from Lake Keuka in New York State, 1912.

Looking ahead to a future yet to be invented: the single-seater and two-seater airborne vehicles conjured up by Albert Robida for his 1893 book *Le Vingtième Siècle* (Editions Georges Decaux).

*The concierge's flat, which in all houses was now situated on the top floor, on the landing pad, to cope with airborne traffic, had been replaced in Philcox Lorris's house – along with the concierge – by an electric panel which provided all the necessary services at the press of a button.*
*An aerocab, which had left the sky-depot on its own and had arrived on its control cable, was already waiting for Georges on the landing pad. Before jumping in, the young man looked at the vast expanse of Paris spread out below, as far as the eye could see, nestling in the valley of the Seine, right out to Fontainebleau beyond the southern suburbs...The sky was already filled with vehicles of all sorts, airship-omnibuses one after another and trying to make up lost time, express-planes from the inter-city or continental services progressing at full speed, aerocabs and aerocoaches milling around tube stations where the trains followed one another almost without pause. To the West a gigantic aero-liner from South America advanced majestically through the haze of a distant mist.*

Albert Robida, Le Vingtième Siècle, *la vie électrique* (Engel, 1890).

### The role of imagination

With little awareness of technical feasibility, writers have been prolix with their futurist visions of machines for combined use in the road and the air: the idea of such dual-purpose devices in fact comfortably pre-dates the invention of both the car and the aeroplane.

In 1846 Frenchman Emile Souvestre, in *Le Monde tel qu'il sera*, made great play of the variety of different flying machines that would throng the skies above large towns: flying hackney-cabs, omnibus-balloons, winged tilburies...

A quarter of a century later the avid American readers of 'dime novels', that pulp fiction sold for a dime (or ten cents) a go, could discover various flying machines in the adventures of the inventor Frank Reade, in stories by Edward F. Ellis and then by Harry Enton and Luis P. Senarens ('Luis No-name') who took over and wrote 191 further Frank Reade stories. During this time, on the other side of the Atlantic the arrangement of our airspace – and the linked vertical development of townscapes – was evoked by the writer and illustrator Albert Robida, without a doubt the greatest visionary of his time.

Airborne combat between flying vehicles: 'The *Petit Swan* succeeds in spearing the rear of the *Remember*' in this illustration by A. Parys from *Les Mangeurs du Feu* by Louis Jacolliot (Marpon and Flammarion, 1887).

*What was the 'Remember'?*
*It wasn't a boat destined solely to cross the Ocean.*
*It wasn't a balloon built expressly to move through the air.*
*It wasn't only some monstrous motor car intended to ride across our roads.*
*Instead it was these three things at the same time. The 'Remember' achieved the definitive conquest of land, air and water.*

*Louis Jacolliot,* Les Mangeurs du Feu
*(Girard & Boite, 1887).*

GARAGE
CHEZ
SOI

'A garage in your home' – or the personal airport. An illustration by René Vincent for *Aéropolis*, a comic novel by Henry Kistemaeckers about life in the air (Librairie Charpentier & Pasquelle, 1909).

Jules Verne created the *Epouvante*, a machine that moved on land, on and under the water, and in the air. In unsafe hands it could prove highly dangerous. This photo-gravure by Maylander is based on an illustration by Georges Roux, and taken from *Maître du Monde* (Hetztel, in the collection *Les Voyages Extraordinaires*, 1904).

*At that moment, in what conditions was the Epouvante making progress?...Having transformed his boat into a car, was the captain to be found on the roads bordering the lake?...If that were the case, and even if I hadn't been made aware of anything for several hours, the machine, if it was being driven at full speed, must surely be a good distance away?...Or maybe, having reverted to a submarine, it was carrying on its journey under the waters of the lake?...*

Jules Verne, Maître du Monde *(Hetzel, 1904).*

The inventor Robur had already designed the *Albatros*, a helicopter propelled by 37 twin-blade rotors. Later he would turn to the *Epouvante*, a vehicle capable of not only taking to the road but also of 'flying with the eagles'. Here it is depicted in another illustration by Georges Roux, in a photo-gravure by E. Duplessis from *Maître du Monde* by Jules Verne (Hetzel, 1904, in the collection *Les Voyages Extraordinaires*).

*The men of this 29th century lived in the midst of a never-ending fairy-tale, without realising their good fortune. Offhand about the marvels of the time, they were unimpressed by those that progress brought them every day. It all seemed natural to them. If they had compared them to the past, they would have appreciated our civilisation better, and would have been aware of the ground covered since then. How much more admirable would seem our modern cities with their 100m-wide streets and 300m-high buildings, always at the same temperature, the sky milling with thousands of aerocars and aero-omnibuses!*

*Jules Verne,* La journée d'un journaliste américain en 2890, *in the* Journal d'Amiens (Moniteur de la Somme), *no21, January 1891.*

Perched on a platform in the centre of Paris, a lady and a young girl prepare to board a taxi-aeroplane. 'I don't envy those who'll be living in 1965,' wrote Albert Robida, referring to his novel *En 1965*. 'They'll be caught up in the cogs of society, mechanised to such a degree that I wonder where they will find the time and the means to savour the joys at one time at our disposition: wandering in the streets, beside the water or in the woods, enjoying calm and solitude. They won't have known them, these joys, so they won't be able to have missed them; but for me, who knows, I feel sorry for them.' This illustration of his was used for the cover of no.1896 of *Les Annales*, for 26 October 1919, the issue containing the story in question.

*Perhaps devices of locomotion equipped with wheels will appear ever-so old-fashioned to those generations who will be present at the dawning of the year 2000...*

*For daily trips there will be nothing more convenient than the runabout balloon. It will be a sort of winged carriage, whose body will hold just enough gas to ensure that the vehicle never gets exceeds an altitude of 10 metres. A small electric machine will actuate a pair of 10m-long aluminium legs articulated like those of a very large bird, and these will imitate trotting or walking motion and transport the balloon at a speed of about 25kph.*

G. Labadie-Lagrave, *Lecture du Dimanche, 4 July 1897, with reference to the* Illustrated English Magazine.

Public transport in the year 2000, as seen in a promotional chromo-lithograph of 1899 from printers Vieillemard.

It would be no problem in 2012 reaching the roof-top of big department stores if you were using a private plane to do your shopping, suggests this 1912 post card publicising Lombard chocolates.

Another publicity postcard for Lombard chocolates, showing a further aspect of life in 2012, the car-aircraft.

In the year 2000, everyone will have their own flying vehicle – that much is certain, according to this second post card of 1899 from Vieillemard.

### The first success: René Tampier's Avion-automobile

Following the example set by Glenn Curtiss, several multi-function machines were attempted in France. The most memorable was René Tampier's Avion-automobile – of which numerous photos were published in the press of the time, showing it travelling down the Grands Boulevards of Paris and in the streets of Montmartre, surrounded by ordinary vehicles.

The starting point was a classic biplane with a fabric fuselage, but with wings that folded back along its length. All that was then necessary was to lock the propeller and unfold a second axle and set of steering controls from the centre of the fuselage. The plane then became a car, but operating 'back-to-front' in that the tail and the folded-back wings were now at the front of the vehicle, necessitating the driver to turn around in the cockpit.

As might be imagined, a plane needed a more powerful engine than a car. Because a shared engine would have posed serious problems, Tampier opted for a twin-engined approach. A 300bhp Hispano-Suiza engine powered the airscrew whilst a four-cylinder 10CV engine looked after the car side, with both engines sharing a common cooling system. There was a disc-type clutch and a three-speed gearbox, with a differential housed in the undercarriage, which was suitably reinforced for high-speed road use. Various modifications and extra items of equipment made the Avion-automobile relatively heavy, but that didn't prevent it being successfully tested on 9 and 10 November 1921, at Buc, just outside Paris. It was under its own steam, too, that it travelled on the road, via Boulogne-sur-Seine, to the Grand Palais in Paris for the Salon de l'Aviation – where it was one of the stars.

The Avion-automobile of René Tampier in flight, November 1921.

Tampier's machine in road-going configuration: the wings are folded back and the pilot has turned around in order to drive 'backwards' on the road.

Paris, 11 November 1921: The Avion-automobile on the
Champs-Elysées heading towards the Grand Palais for
the 7th international aeronautical exhibition.

The specialist press was enthusiastic. The limited space the machine took up when its wings were folded was presented as a valuable advantage for garaging it, or for long-distance transport or even for use aboard warships. After a forced landing, the Avion-automobile could in theory remain mobile, in its car format. It could follow the cavalry, the self-propelled guns and the car-borne artillery in their engagements. Manoeuvering around airstrips would be easier. Finally, the second engine could serve as an auxiliary power unit for heating, lighting, ventilation, starting the main engine, and so on...

But perhaps because, after the end of the First World War, the machine was seen above all as having a military rôle, it was rapidly abandoned, in what were supposedly more peaceable times. As will be seen throughout this book, it was hugely influential, the ideas of Tampier being widely copied.

### The concept of the mobile wing and 'modified planes'

In 1926 an American, Else H. Tubbe, took up the general ideas of René Tampier and lodged an eight-page patent describing his 'Airplane', a machine that was original and (at least on paper) a dozen years ahead of its time.

The central element of the Airplane was a cabin big enough to accommodate several passengers and equipped with three wheels, two at the front. A large-diameter propeller was mounted at the rear of the cabin, overhanging a very low tailplane, and a long straight wing was fixed on top. The innovatory aspect of the machine – other than its looks, which anticipated future prototype flying-cars – was that the bloc comprising the wing and the prop pivoted 90 degrees to align with the cabin. In this format it could easily be used on the road and even in town.

The idea of the movable wing continued to gain a following and was soon proved to be a viable concept. At the end of the 1920s George G. Spratt took to the air in his Car-plane, a machine with a single pivoting 'turnable wing' similar to that on Tubbe's machine. Spratt carried on his researches and was in the news a few years later, in 1939, when he developed a flying boat, the Spratt 107 or Controlwing.

A newspaper article on this attracted the notice of automotive and aeronautical engineer William B. Stout, then working on the Skycar project – which, despite its name, was in the beginning purely an aircraft. In 1944 the two men developed the Convair 103 (also known as the Skycar IV or the Spratt-Stout Model 8) for the research division of Consolidated Vultee that Stout then headed. This was a plane that was road-usable, in that its wing could be detached and left at the airfield. In spite of its weight (the wing alone weighed more than 2cwt), the

### Road-going plane or flying car?

While the (rare) post-war French inventors generically called their machine an aérauto, the Americans used the two separate denominations of 'roadable aircraft' and 'flying auto' – depending on whether it was more a plane modified to be used on the ground or a car given additional equipment to allow it to take to the air. Thus James Wisner Holland's Ercoupe, for example, is a pure 'roadable aircraft'. In 1949 Holland modified a popular two-seat aircraft of the time so it could be used on the road: the wings unbolted and could be stowed on top of the fuselage. On the other hand the Ford Pinto on which Henry Smolinski managed to fix the wings, twin-boom tail assembly and rear engine of a regular Cessna Skymaster – without specific modifications – is the perfect expression of the term 'flying car'.

If this difference in approach cannot be justified on this side of the Atlantic, this is because for historical and above all geographical reasons European countries have never regarded the aeroplane as a common – banal, even – means of transport, as in the United States. The American psyche is nourished by the idea of wide-open spaces and the myth of a new frontier that has to be pushed back ceaselessly. Furthermore, Americans are convinced that there is nothing more important than their personal liberty. So there is nothing extraordinary about the annexing of the private aeroplane as a tool to extend their ability to travel.

So, flying car or road-going plane? Everyone has his preferences. The key thing is that such a machine should not only be able to fly but also to use the roads as a true dual-function device. If that is not the case, then all you're left with is a sort of private flying-saucer.

James W. Holland's Ercoupe of 1949, as depicted in *Atomes* no.51 of June 1950: more of a modified aircraft than a true flying car. The machine could manage 110mph in the air and 45mph on the road.

machine made numerous successful flights in the hands of test-pilot Bob Townsend, who recommended that work continue. A series of modifications was carried out and the aircraft, significantly reduced in weight, was found to have much improved handling. In this form it flew back and forth between Nashville and San Diego, the company HQ, to undergo other tests, all technically conclusive.

Despite this, in 1947 George Spratt arrived at the end of his contract and returned home to Connecticut to concentrate – as Glenn Curtiss before him – on the development of an amphibian version of his plane. This went through various incarnations right up until the 1970s. As for the Convair 103, it received no further development, and stayed at the prototype stage: Consolidated Vultee had other projects for a totally different flying car, developed by engineer Theodore P. Hall (see Chapter 5).

In parallel with Spratt's first experiments, the early 1930s saw the development of several planes along traditional lines, with a front-mounted prop, a two-wheel front axle and a single tail-wheel but with

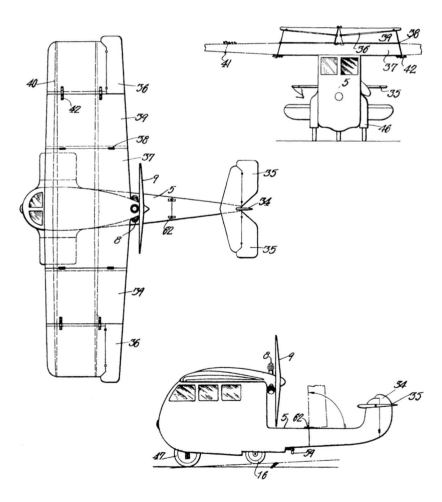

Else H. Tubbe's 1926 patent application for his 'Airplane'.

wings that folded to the rear, to join at their ends above and overhanging the tail. These were modified planes, however, rather than flying cars in the strict sense of the word. One example was the 'Airplane' of William N. Helsch, which was the object of a patent application in 1930 and was built the following year. However, whether the tests were satisfactory or not, nothing more was heard of the machine.

There is little doubt that numerous projects were developed in the first third of the 20th century by inventors who for the most part worked with unshakable determination but largely on their own. History has not been fair in only retaining the names of those few who made the effort to apply for patents or who presented their machines at air shows – something which has at least allowed some photos to survive.

One of the most famous amongst this assemblage of merry eccentrics was Waldo Waterman, inventor of the Arrowbile, the first flying car worthy of that name...in that it actually flew.

The Convair 103 (NX22448) developed by William B. Stout and George G. Spratt for Consolidated Vultee, in 1944: the wing unbolted and the machine could then take to the road as a car, capable of 50mph. In flight, the Convair was claimed to be capable of 110mph.

Waldo Warerman's Aerobile (N-54P) in 1957, ready to
take off into the Californian skies.

# 2

# Waldo Waterman: from the Whatsit to the Aerobile

From the end of the 1920s it seemed certain that after having bought his car every upstanding citizen would next find himself behind the controls of his own private plane. Initiatives to develop ultra-cheap machines blossomed as a result. But one man, Waldo Waterman, rose to an even more unbelievable challenge, that of the flying car.

## A turbulent childhood

Waldo Waterman was born on 16 June 1894 in San Diego, in southern California. From his youngest days he was interested in the world of aviation, then making its first hesitant steps. His heroes were the Wright brothers, the first to have mastered powered flight, and Glenn Curtiss, without any doubt the best-known and most admired American aviator in those pioneer times.

In 1909 an article in *Popular Mechanics* led the young Waldo to build a glider, at the controls of which he launched himself from the top of a canyon. He was 15 years old. The following year he built a second plane, with the help of friend Kenneth Kendall. The machine had so little power that it had to be towed by a car before it could take off. After a few flights it crashed, leaving its young pilot with two broken ankles.

Whilst continuing his education at San Diego High School, Waldo Waterman was lucky enough to meet his idol, Glenn Curtiss, who had set up base for the winter on North Island. He was even on occasion able to work for Curtiss, and in February 1911 he witnessed the first flight of a new sea-plane, the Curtiss Triad. The machine took off from the waters of the bay, lowered its undercarriage in flight, and landed without drama on a runway a little further away. The trial was a modest one, but then these were early days for these bizarre planes – all stomach, with a fuselage like the hull of a boat and an undercarriage comprising floats as well as wheels. So this was no small feat. At the end of one of these flights Curtiss exclaimed "If only we could take to the roads as well, just as if we were in a car, then we'd really have something!" The young Waldo took this remark at face value. Slowly but surely the idea of a flying machine that could be converted into a car started to germinate. Glenn Curtiss, of course, would undertake just such a project himself, with his Autoplane, as already discussed in the preceding chapter.

## A career in aviation

The following year Waldo Waterman left San Diego High School and in September started at the University of Berkeley, studying aeronautical engineering. When the US entered the war he was spared military service because of the weak state of his ankles, and ended up in the US Army Signal Corps School of Military Aeronautics, where he taught the theory of flight. Next he worked for the US Aircraft Corporation, which had just won a contract to build 100 examples of the JN or 'Jenny', a biplane developed by the Curtiss Aeroplane Company and which in JN-4 form became the most famous US plane of the First World War. At the end of the war Waterman was charged with closing down the business. He profited from this to acquire part of the company's stock and equipment and he set up shop in the Santa Monica region, a small town west of Los Angeles that served as the seafront for the capital of southern California.

The Waterman Aircraft Manufacturing Company began by making gliders, but business became difficult when the government dumped large numbers of aircraft on the market, their prices slashed to 10% of their value. In 1927, therefore, Waldo Waterman joined the team of engineers at the Bach Aircraft Company in Santa Monica, the firm then being in the process of developing a lightweight three-engined cargo plane. The next year he directed the building of the Los Angeles Metropolitan Airport – today Van Nuys Airport – before taking over its running. A road leading to the airport today bears his name; at the airport you can still see the hangar that appeared in the last scene of the film *Casablanca*.

Between times, Waterman won the 1929 Air Transport Race – part of Cleveland's National Air Races – in a machine built by the Bach Aircraft Company. The following year he became world-record holder for flying at altitude, at the controls of a plane carrying a cargo of a ton.

In 1930, while he was in charge of closing down Bach, which had failed to weather the Wall Street Crash of 1929 – and in the midst of his many other activities – Waldo Waterman started pondering again on the dreams of his youth. Before long the first plans for the Waterman Whatsit would emerge.

**The Whatsit**

Imagine a large egg-like glazed cabin with a propeller at the back and a single wheel at the front, fixed on top of a massive vee-shaped wing with a wheel at either end – in other words something a bit like a giant boomerang – and you have a rough idea of the lumpen lines of the Whatsit. Look beyond the bizarre appearance, however, and what you had was in fact America's first flying wing. Given all this, there was nothing strange about the name, chosen in reference to the astonishment the machine provoked when first seen in public.

Not being transformable, the machine wasn't suitable for road use: in Waterman's mind it was a prototype of a small plane that would be easy for each and everyone to pilot and, above all, a stepping stone towards the creation of a flying car.

The Whatsit underwent testing from March 1932 onwards, at Los Angeles Metropolitan Airport. Several fruitless attempts took place in April and May, with Waterman at the controls. In the course of one of them, the front wheel got stuck in a gopher's hole, these rodents being a noted pest in the region. The next time, the machine took off without incident but suddenly dropped earthwards when only airborne by a

*Aerocars are omnipresent...*

A.G. Stangland, The Ancient Brain, *in* Science Wonder Stories, *October 1929.*

In 1935, Alain Saint-Ogan depicted *Zig et Puce au XXIe siècle* – a period when road-going aircraft would be seen as a normal mode of transport.

Waldo Waterman's experimental flying wing, the
Whatsit (X12272). The inventor poses by the nose in
this photo from 1 March 1934. Restored by Waterman,
the Whatsit would be offered to the Smithsonian
National Air and Space Museum in Washington in 1950.

few feet. Waterman managed to do a pancake landing without injuring himself, despite the plane ending up on its roof – thankfully the cabin was remarkably strong. During October, another test ended again in failure: this time the Whatsit, with another pilot at the controls, was more seriously damaged and Waterman decided to put the machine into store for a while.

During 1933 other test flights took place, highlighting several design flaws, but lack of finances meant Waterman had to call a halt to the project. He knew how to bounce back. He returned to his previous field of activity, creating aerodromes and opening new airlines, before becoming a commercial pilot for a while, in particular for Transcontinental and Western Air – better known as TWA – on the Los Angeles to San Francisco route.

## A new challenge for Henry Ford

During the previous decade the idea of every American having his own private plane rapidly gained ground – to the point of appearing, at the beginning of the thirties, as a veritable necessity of life. This wasn't a new idea. According to Pierre Versins, founder of the Maison d'Ailleurs museum of science-fiction, at Yverdon in Switzerland, and a historian of futurist literature, it appeared for the first time in *A jövo" század regénye* (*'A Novel of the Next Century'*). This was a story by the Hungarian author Mor Jokai, published in instalments between 1872 and 1874. Translated into German, but never published in French or English, the work didn't have the impact it deserved.

An aircraft for everyone sounded indeed like something right up the street of Henry Ford, the man who had dreamt of offering every American a car – and had done so much to achieve this – and whose son Edsel was a flying enthusiast. In fact, the car-maker did rise to the challenge, and his designers worked on a pocket-sized aeroplane, the Flying Flivver, of which three versions were built and tested, starting in 1926. Unfortunately, in 1928 a friend of Ford's, test-pilot Harry Brooks, died in an accident when the third prototype crashed on a Miami beach. The project was definitively abandoned.

## A 'New Deal' for aviation

The election of Franklin Delano Roosevelt to the US presidency in 1932 and the arrival of a new administration, more dynamic and more attuned to the future, revived interest in the private plane.

In 1933 a brief to study the question was given to Olympic athlete and former military pilot Eugene Vidal – father of writer Gore Vidal. At the time Vidal headed the federal Department of Commerce's Aeronautics Branch, to be renamed in 1934 the Bureau of Air Commerce. In November

*1999 is overwhelmingly a flying culture, with privately owned antigravity space cars and public space buses that follow prescribed routes.*

Bob Olsen, Flight in 1999, *in* Air Wonder Stories, *September 1929.*

Waldo Waterman's first Arrowbile (X262Y), in 1937.

1933 he organised the nationwide Vidal Safety Airplane Competition. The object was the development of a safe and easy-to-pilot plane for the general public, with low costs of purchase and maintenance – its price was fixed at less than $700, or roughly the cost of a mid-range car and about $500 cheaper than the small planes then on the market.

In August 1934 Vidal appraised the thirty or so projects submitted. Just one came from an established aircraft maker, as such companies didn't want internal competition to their own more expensive planes. Consequently the rest were the work of small firms and independent hobbyists, some not very serious. A few projects stood out, however, in particular that of the Hammond company of Ypsilanti, Michigan, and the AC-35 Autogiro submitted by Harold Pitcairn. There was also a truly out-of-the-ordinary machine put forward by a certain Waldo Waterman, derived from the Whatsit and prompted by the competition's aims being similar to what he had been trying to achieve for some years. Funds were allocated to several of these inventors to develop prototypes of the most interesting projects, so they could be presented as soon as possible.

### From the Arrowplane to the Aerobile

For his new venture Waterman decided to keep the single vee-shaped wing, with its arrowhead configuration – hence the name Arrowplane. As with the Whatsit, the machine also had a rear-mounted propeller behind the cabin. But Waterman had learnt his lesson from the poor weight distribution of the Whatsit, and this time the cabin sat directly under the wing. The Arrowplane had no tail unit and was thus again a flying wing. With a 95bhp four-cylinder Menasco engine it was – at least on paper – a revolutionary machine of highly individual appearance.

Built in a record time in the course of May 1935 and swiftly put through its initial testing, the Arrowplane flew from Santa Monica to Washington DC. There, in July, it was presented to the Bureau of Air Commerce, which declared it in conformity with the criteria of the competition – except in its calculated on-sale price, which clearly exceeded the $700 limit that had been set. This had in any case been deemed unachievable by all the contestants. A little later Hammond's machine was also declared in conformity with the rules of the contest.

Buoyed by this success, Waterman created a new firm, The Waterman Arrowplane Corporation, based in Santa Monica. But he didn't want to put the Arrowplane into series production. Profiting from the publicity generated by the machine, he devoted himself instead to reviving his old project of a flying car. After all, if the general public was ready to buy a private plane, it would be just as open – if not more – to the idea of buying the same sort of plane if into the bargain it could be converted into an automobile.

The first modification carried out to the Arrowplane consisted in making the wing detachable – and in making the wheels of the

*London is now a collection of huge skyscrapers, among which are monorails and aerocabs.*

Anon., The Time Traveller, *in Scoops, 3 March 1934.*

resultant 'car' section take the drive. To keep production costs as low as possible, Waterman decided to use as many existing car parts as possible. Thus the radiator and the steering came from a Ford and the steering wheel from an American Austin (the US-built version of the Austin Seven), while the headlamp, the differential and the brakes came from a Willys. The need for a lightweight power unit led Waterman to choose a 100bhp Studebaker engine, and later he adopted items of interior trim and the radiator grille of the Studebaker. It was hardly surprising that the machine in its later versions ended up looking like a cross between an Arrowplane and a Studebaker. Only the aircraft equipment was expensive; the magnetic compass, the altimeter and the air-speed gauge.

The machine comprised two parts. The car part had three wheels in aerodynamic fairings, two driven rear wheels, a rear-mounted prop, and a single headlamp – a configuration that in Californian law made it a motorcycle. The aircraft part comprised two wings that formed a vee and which could be unbolted in a few moments and left at the airport.

The first successful flight took place on 21 February 1937, with Waldo Waterman as usual at the controls. Everything went well. For the time the performance of the Arrowbile was on the money: 125mph in the air and 70mph on the road, with a fuel consumption of approaching 19mpg.

1 Out of Waldo D. Waterman's garage, his Arrowbile is wheeled. It is more convenient and less expensive to keep the plane in the family garage than in a hangar. Daughter Jane is at the wheel.

2 Down to the airport goes Arrowbile, a wingless, three-wheeled auto, engine driving wheels instead of propeller.

3 At the hangar, the wings are lowered and attached firmly to the body. Waterman has seven Arrowbiles under construction, five of them ordered by Studebaker whose engines power this plane.

4 The Arrowbile races down the airport runway. Its engine is now linked to propeller which, the plane being a "pusher," is in rear.

5 The Arrowbile takes off. A curious-looking machine, it is made mostly of automobile parts. It has a Studebaker engine and generator, Willys-Overland brakes and differential, Ford steering assembly, battery and radiator.

6 In flight along the coast (above), the Arrowbile has a top speed of 120 m.p.h., can carry two passengers 350 miles. Its price is $3,000.

*Life* magazine of 16 August 1937 devoted a full page to the Arrowbile. At the controls is Jane Waterman, daughter of Waldo: there was no doubt that aviation for everyman was just around the corner!

This was all a long way from the cheap machine dreamt of by Vidal a few years previously, but no matter: it was the first successful test flight of a true flying car, conceived as such. In the wake of this success, an agreement for the supply of parts was concluded between Waterman and the Studebaker Corporation, which placed an order for five machines.

In 1938, before beginning its crossing of the North American continent, Arrowbile no.3 is baptised 'Miss South Bend' at Clover Field (Santa Monica, California) by Dorothy Hoffman, wife of Studebaker Corporation president Paul Hoffman.

## A flotilla of Arrowbiles

Machines 2 and 3 were built and tested at the beginning of 1938, with the others in the process of assembly. The first three Arrowbiles left the Santa Monica works by air for New York. To garner publicity various stopovers were planned, including Cleveland, where the machines were to participate in the National Air Races, a gigantic air show organised over the Labor Day weekend in early September.

However on the way Arrowbile 1 was forced to land in Arizona and was severely damaged; the pilot admitted he wasn't used to flying the machine. Then Arrowbile 2 had to break its journey in Indiana for mechanical reasons. The success of the venture therefore hinged on the last machine and its pilot, Jerry Phillips. After five forced landings

Jerry Phillips, the pilot of Waterman Arrowbile no.3
('Miss South Bend'), talks to service-station staff about
the machine, in the course of his 1938 crossing of the
United States. The six-cylinder Studebaker engine
used regular petrol.

and a number of technical incidents that nearly cost him his life, he eventually completed the long trip, but was not able to fly at an altitude higher than 6,500ft or at a speed in excess of 90mph.

The final leg, not far from New York, ended in a field. The Arrowbile needed serious repairs before it could take to the air again, but the press was awaiting the triumphant arrival of the flying car the same day a good few miles away. The pilot, with the aid of a local farmer, transported the wings on the back of his lorry, and they made it to the rendez-vous and put the machine back together just before the media arrived.

By the skin of its teeth the Arrowbile had won its bet, and would be the star of the New York Automobile Show that year. The machine next made its way to South Bend, home of Studebaker, to be modified according to the recommendations of Jerry Phillips, who felt amongst other things that it was too heavy for its engine power.

But the Arrowbile had another weakness – an important one. Its costs of production had been poorly calculated. A retail price of $3,000 had been trumpeted, yet there was no way the Arrowbile could be made for anything less than $7,000 a time. That was very expensive. Even for a vehicle that promised to make the highway a thing of the past, Studebaker judged the Arrowbile not to be financially viable and decided to cancel its involvement in the project. A fourth example was built, re-using the wings of the first prototype and with several modifications including a widened undercarriage, but it was purely a plane rather than a flying car.

In a further turn of bad luck, Waldo Waterman's other financial backer, former TWA director Harris M. Hanshue, died suddenly the same year. Then the inventor was laid low by acute appendicitis and was seriously ill for several months. Unable to put his finances on a firm footing, Waterman was forced to suspend his activities.

### The Aerobile

At the beginning of the 1940s Waldo Waterman bought back the remains of Arrowbile 4 from Studebaker, along with some other surviving parts, with a view to building some new machines – although not necessarily flying cars. After having organised training programmes for pilots at Pasadena Junior College, Waterman was awarded a one-year contract as chief engineer in the research department of Consolidated Vultee in Detroit, where he worked with William B. Stout, who was also a fan of flying cars. But Waterman's project was anything but a priority, because the US had joined the war and above all needed fighter planes. In any case, Stout was more interested in other projects for flying cars, working with William Chana and George Spratt, with whom he developed the Convair 103 (see Chapter 1). Waterman therefore went home to California.

His last flying car was laid down in 1947. But as he only worked in his spare time, it took ten years to complete what he now called the

*I thus had the opportunity, on several occasions, to see amphibious planes take off with difficulty from the water. One day more than another this really struck me and I thought of the almost certain benefit there would be in equipping these heavy birds with rotating floats...It was just a step from there to imagine that having proceeded to the ad-hoc construction of these floats – or rather, these wheels – aeroplanes so equipped would not only get around on the water more easily but could also just as well land on the shore, even run along it and perhaps take off from it.*

*Raymond Desorties, Le 'Tétrabie', Gallimard, 1933.*

Aerobile (or No.6), a three-seater registered N54P. The Studebaker power unit had given way to a flat-six aero-engine bought after the collapse of the Tucker Automobile Company, which had used the unit, converted from air-cooling to water-cooling, in the ill-fated rear-engined Tucker Torpedo. The wing of the plane, which had previously unbolted in two parts, was now a one-piece unit.

In May 1957 the Aerobile made a successful maiden flight. But it was clear that there was no market for such a machine. The adventure of the flying car was over for Waldo Waterman. There had been too little time to develop viable prototypes when his researches had financial backing, and then several turns of bad luck had put paid to his hopes of selling a hybrid vehicle. Even when his dreams had become reality, that reality had proved fragile.

In March 1961, repainted in Buick Blue, the Aerobile was offered to the National Air and Space Museum in Washington. Waldo Waterman, who died in 1976, remains, however, a legendary figure and a reference in the world of aviation – and not just for fans of flying cars.

The Aerobile with its flying part removed. The machine is today the property of the Smithsonian National Air and Space Museum in Washington.

With his ultra-futurist artwork, illustrator Arthur Charles Radebaugh often stunned business customers such as Chrysler or Coca-Cola. Here, at the beginning of the 1950s, he drew up a flying car that was distinctive to say the least, and clearly seen as being used by the average American. The client for the image is not known, and the original artwork has today disappeared.

Pitcairn Autogiro Company's Pitcairn PA-36 was capable of vertical take-off, and could thus in theory offer competition to the helicopter. History proved otherwise.

The Pitcairn PA-36 Whirl Wing autogyro, developed in 1938 by Harold F. Pitcairn, was a military version of the AC-35. Once its rotors had been folded, the machine was perfectly usable on the road.

## The Pitcairn AC-35 and other autogyros

In the second half of the 1930s there were several projects for lightweight autogyros able to be modified for open-road or urban use. The best-known remains the Pitcairn AC-35, which was entered in Vidal's competition alongside the Arrowplane.

The autogyro was originally conceived and developed by a British company, the Cierva Autogiro Company Ltd. Unlike a helicopter, on an autogyro the rotor is not powered by the engine but turns by auto-rotation – in other words of its own accord. The machine therefore needs another means of propulsion, this in general being a front-mounted propeller.

At the beginning of the decade Harold F. Pitcairn, who had trained at the Glenn Curtiss flying school in Newport and was a pioneer of air mail in the US, became the Cierva licencee for the United States. He duly founded the Pitcairn Autogiro Company, and in 1932 he began to develop a small two-seat autogyro that would be easy to pilot. Tests of the PA-22 went on for two years, with success, and in 1934 the Experimental Development department of the Bureau of Air Commerce decided to subsidise a programme for a more technically evolved version.

This soon saw the light of day thanks to the Autogiro Company of America, a division of the Pitcairn Autogiro Company set up in order to develop new models and then sell design rights. The new Pitcairn AC-35 had its engine at the rear of a three-wheeled cabin, and was topped by a three-blade folding rotor, with two easily-removable co-axial props at the front. These proved too noisy and were soon replaced by a single airscrew in a redesigned front end. In this form the AC-35 was usable on the road, once its rotor blades had been folded, thanks to its single driven rear wheel. On 2 October 1936 the vice-president of the Autogiro Company of America, James G. Ray, landed the experimental model in a Washington park before driving it to the federal Department of Commerce.

Whether or not a road-going version would ultimately emerge, the autogyro seemed perfectly adapted to urban use. Ideal for those in the suburbs, it could be landed on a pocket handkerchief, could winnow its way through anywhere, and could be stored in a corner of one's garage. Tests continued, but the AC-35 wasn't the expected success. Not helping matters, in 1936 the machine's inventor, the Spaniard Juan de la Cierva, died in an airline accident, and with him the autogyro lost its principal advocate.

Furthermore, in Europe a war was brewing and Germany wanted to prove its superiority to the world. In February 1938 famed aviatrix and Nazi party favourite Hanna Reitsch demonstrated the swastika-emblazoned Focke-Achgelis Fa 61 helicopter in Berlin for 14 nights in a row, flying it inside a covered athletics stadium. The press was astounded, and henceforth the helicopter was regarded as a more viable way forward than the autogyro.

Pitcairn subsequently developed the Pitcairn PA-36 Whirl Wing, an all-metal military version of the AC-35, and like it also transformable for road use. It was too late, however: military grants for the research, development and production of rotor-equipped machines were now going to the construction of helicopters rather than autogyros. Neither the AC-36 nor the AC-35 would ever reach the market, and the Pitcairn AC-35 ended up with Waldo Waterman's Aerobile in the National Air and Space Museum in Washington.

An interesting variation on the autogyro theme was the machine conceived by W.F. Gerhardt and the object of a patent application in 1937. Technically it was classic autogyro, but its design was extremely modern. With three cowled wheels, its egg-shaped cabin harked forward to the Italian Isetta bubble-car of the 1950s. But unlike the Isetta, Gerhardt's autogyro remained a paper dream.

Much later, in the mid-fifties, the autogyro was revived in the form of an ultra-light leisure-orientated machine, the Gyrocopter of Igor Bensen. This type of machine has not yet had the last word in the battle with the 'regular' flying car: the CarterCopter (see Chapter 12) could still have a bright future in front of it.

According to the magazine *Science et Vie* (no.343, April 1946), the helicopter 'will in the future serve as an airborne taxi to take passengers of the big airlines from the airport to their destination in town, and as a private plane to take tourists to the countryside without their having to struggle on crowded roads, landing and taking off using the smallest patches of ground'. The illustration is by well-known French artist René Ravo.

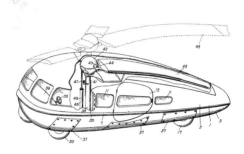

In 1951 Wilber L. Masterton lodged a patent for a smart-looking 'Land, Sea and Air Plane'. The machine was a sort of helicopter with a single driven rear wheel and rotors that stowed in the top of the fuselage. It never left the drawing board.

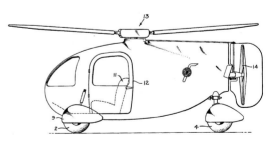

W.F. Gerhardt's 1937 patent application for an autogyro convertible into a car.

The Roadable Airplane of Theodore P. Hall ready for
take-off in 1939.

**3.**

# Integration and modularity

In the second half of the 1930s the flying car moved away from a concept based principally on the private plane, to become a genuinely hybrid machine. At the same time two different visions emerged of the form this new type of vehicle should take.

## Two radically different approaches

By the 1930s a flying car was seen as having to be truly dual-purpose. It had to fulfil all the functions expected of any aircraft in its category (sufficient flight range, moderate running and maintenance costs, ability to land pretty much anywhere) and at the same time not demand over-much pilot instruction; equally it had to be usable as a small motor car, whether on the open road or in town, which implied a modest size and a certain robustness. If the car part of most such machines remained a relatively orthodox small saloon, mostly a three-wheeler with – in many cases – a fixed propeller mounted behind the cabin, when it came to the flying part there were strong divergences in concept, with two schools of thought standing out.

On the one hand there was what could be termed an integrated flying system: a permanently-constituted aircraft made up of a car equipped with an engine and propeller at the rear, and topped by a single folding wing which would either pivot in one movement to align with the fuselage or have two separate points of articulation.

On the other hand was the modular approach, whereby a small car had an entirely independent flying element attached to it – wing, rear fuselage, tailplane and fins, engine and propeller. This was designed to be suitably easy to unbolt, and the user, once back on the ground, could leave it at an aerodrome or else take it away on a trailer, making this modular version every bit as practical as an integrated machine.

At the end of the thirties it was taken for granted that there was strong potential for a dual-purpose land-and-air machine, and several inventors worked assiduously on the idea, with followers of both the integrated system and the modular system launching into the construction of prototypes.

### An 'all-in-one': The Plane-Mobile of Zuck and Whitaker

In 1931 Daniel R. Zuck was a farmer near Lancaster in Pennsylvania. He was plane-lover and in his spare time he built gliders. As the only technical documentation he had was photographs in specialist magazines, the results he achieved were often more than a little disappointing – and even downright dangerous. But the young man had been bitten by the flying bug and he abandoned working the land to take a course at the Casey Jones School of Aeronautics, while signing on for three years as a mechanic at Newark airport in order to pay for his studies. At the same time he began to design the machine he had dreamed about for several years and for which he already had a name – the Plane-Mobile.

On paper it was a reasonably successful aesthetic compromise between a streamlined saloon and a light plane. The cabin was spacious and there were four wheels – later reduced to three. At the rear was a

triple-blade propeller, although this was subsequently abandoned in favour of a classic front-propeller configuration. There was a long rear fuselage with a twin-fin tailplane, and air brakes were later added to this. The specification, indeed, was constantly changing, as Zuck was forever modifying his drawings. The only thing that didn't change was the pair of wings attached to the top of the fuselage. They were particularly distinctive. This was firstly in terms of their shape: profiled like the wings of a gull, their central part was much thicker and twice as wide as the tips and the section adjoining the fuselage. Secondly, they were articulated using an extremely clever mechanism. Once the Plane-Mobile was on the ground the wings were designed to be folded

Half-car and half-aircraft, the 'Kangaroo Car' had a propeller and an aircraft engine, and travelled on its two rear wheels. All it was missing was a set of wings... (*Popular Science*, May 1937; illustration by Edgar F. Wittmack).

back and simply stacked one on top of the other on top of the fuselage. This operation would transform the machine into a car usable on the open road or in town.

In 1936 Daniel Zuck found work in Los Angeles, in an aircraft factory, and it was there that he met another flying enthusiast, Stanley D. Whitaker, from Spokane. The two men hit it off and decided to pool their efforts. Over several years they worked together to build a prototype that was forever being improved but which never reached the point of being flown. The problem was always the same: weight. Notwithstanding this, in January 1939 a patent was filed concerning the folding system for the wings. Several patents of this type had been registered since the previous decade, but intended more for light aircraft, while in France

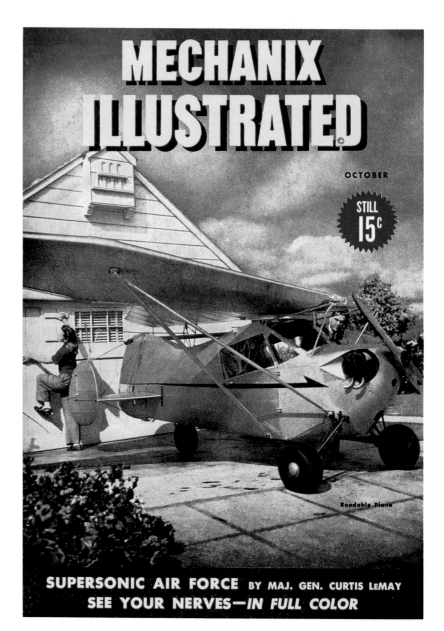

The Plane-Mobile of Daniel Zuck and Stanley Whitaker made the cover of *Mechanix Illustrated* (vol XXXVI, no.6) in October 1946. It could leave a suburban garage by road, at speeds of up to 40mph, before taking to the air and attaining up to 80mph.

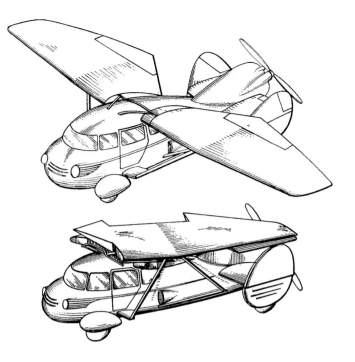

A patent applied for in 1949 by Daniel Zuck shows an alternative version of the Plane-Mobile with the propeller at the rear but with the wings still stacking on the fuselage. The design was more harmonious than the Plane-Mobile but it never saw the light of day.

the Tampier Avion-automobile used a similar approach. But Zuck's system was genuinely something new, in that it was the only one to propose stacking wings, as opposed to wings that folded against the fuselage sides.

A lack of money and the arrival of the Second World War meant that Zuck and Whitaker, in company with their rival Waterman, had to stop work in the early 1940s.

They took up tools at the end of the war and in 1946 the carried out the first conclusive tests of their Plane-Mobile on the dry lake in the Mojave desert. The machine proved reliable, and easy to fly and drive, with performance that was perfectly acceptable. The press devoted numerous enthusiastic articles to it, and Zuck and Whitaker started to plan a more powerful version. But the first Plane-Mobile had already cost them more than $800, a considerable sum at the time, and the small matter of 10,000 hours of work. Added to which, other serious flying-car projects had appeared in the interim, such as Robert Fulton's Airphibian. Finally, no plane-maker was interested in making the Plane-Mobile. As a result of all this, it never reached the production stage.

In 1958 Daniel Zuck published the book *An Airplane in Every Garage*, in which he propagandised for the flying car, likening the ordinary family saloon to the dodo, the mythical bird that became extinct because it was unable to fly. But in spite of a long – and fictitious – passage where Zuck describes his family holidays and how they were made possible by his wonder-machine, and despite a chapter entitled 'Meeting the Russian threat with the Rodable Plane' nobody really paid much attention to him.

[Continued on page 165]

According to its designers the Plane-Mobile could be transformed from car to aeroplane in the twinkling of an eye, as demonstrated for the journalists of *Mechanix Illustrated*.

An 'all-in-one' drawn up by Richard H. Arib in 1942 for his employer, Republic Aviation (RA) and re-touched in 1948. Convinced that after the war the market for flying machines for the general public would take off with a bang, RA envisaged offering this 'Sport Craft Commuter Airplane'.

A magnificent modular machine created by an unknown artist signing himself 'R. Ring'. The illustration probably dates from the end of the 1930s.

A flying car being used for poaching. Drawing by Joseph Hémard for a 1947 diary printed by E. Desfossés.

Another illustration by Hémard for the same diary shows a flying swordfish with the passenger in a swing, a rocket ridden like a horse, a flying car, and a stove on wheels – all part of the imagined motoring scene in 1995.

*Remember what I am going to tell you: a combination of the plane and the car will see the light of day. You may smile. But it will come...*

*Henry Ford, president of the Ford Motor Company, 1940.*

Theodore P. Hall's Roadable Airplane (NX14993) in the California skies, 1939.

### Going 'modular': the Roadable Airplane of Theodore P. Hall

In 1937 Theodore P. Hall was in charge of new-project development for San Diego aircraft maker Consolidated Vultee. With a degree from the famous Massachusetts Institute of Technology, this brilliant engineer already had to his credit design work on such notably successful planes as the PBY Catalina flying-boat and the B24 Liberator bomber.

On a human level, his friends remember him as a perfect gentleman. Tall and elegant and capable of keeping his calm in all circumstances, Hall was above all someone enormously methodical. As a born optimist, he delighted in repeating to his colleagues that for every technical problem, however complex, there was a solution.

After considering the various flying-car projects that were on the go – whether in the air or on paper – Hall came to the conclusion that the interdependence of the control systems for both air and road operations brought with it serious dangers: first of all in the event of a breakdown but equally because of the complexity of operating unfamiliar controls. Hall therefore worked on the theory of modularity. He defined the modular flying car as a machine comprising a road-going component and a flying component, each one if possible having its own engine and its own control and instrumentation systems. As well as increasing the machine's safety and making it easier to fly, the complete independence of the two elements would enormously simplify the processes of coupling and uncoupling.

Theodore Hall didn't delay in putting his ideas into practice. In his spare time, in a hangar at the small Linda Vista aerodrome, he built several versions of a flying car. The first test flights took place in 1939 and continued until 1941. Called the Roadable Airplane, the machine had three wheels – one at the front and two driven wheels at the rear – and a propeller poking through the nose. This body was topped by a single wing of 33ft (10m) span, with a twin-boom tail assembly carrying the tailplane and its two fins, the whole assembly sitting on top of the car like a lid. Fitted with a 95bhp Mercury V8, the machine managed 110mph in flight and could take off or land in only 100 yards. According to Hall, the wings and the twin-boom tail could be unbolted in only four minutes, using an adjustable spanner. In fact you initially needed two people to carry out the conversion, and that clearly took more time. But the system was improved over the years.

Theodore P. Hall was above all a designer of military planes, and the German conquest of Europe and the evident expansionism

of Japan in the Pacific convinced him that the United States would inevitably be dragged into the war. So all the while that he was building the Roadable Airplane he was aware of its military possibilities: it would be easy to mount a machine-gun at the front and the machine could also carry a decent amount of munitions. But the army didn't take up his offer.

The Roadable Airplane seemed to have everything going for it. However, no effort was made to put it on sale. With war declared, priorities in the aeronautical industry changed and the Roadable Airplane – which at the time was covered by no patents – had the same fate as the contemporary Arrowbile, and ended up in a museum. Unfortunately in 1978 the San Diego Aerospace Museum burnt down, and with it perished the Roadable Airplane.

The Roadable Airplane inspired the design of the Hall Flying Car that Ted Hall was to build after the end of the Second World War, as described in Chapter 5.

In 1938 John A. Johnson lodged a patent for this modular 'Autoplane'.

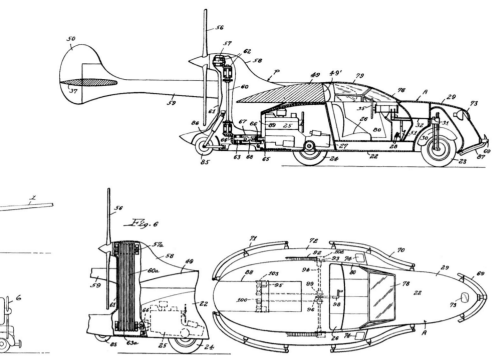

1943 patent application by Frank F. Frakes for a modular flying car.

## The apparent supremacy of the modular system

At the same time other projects for modular vehicles were under study. That of a certain Frank F. Frakes was by far the most impressive – at least visually speaking and if one makes a serious leap of the imagination, as it only ever existed as a series of sketches accompanying the patent application of 1943. It comprised an immense twin-prop aircraft section with the single wing equipped with two engine nacelles of a size suggesting enough power to put into the air any saloon car you could have chosen.

Having by all evidence been the object of a great deal more thought, the Autoplane proposed by John A. Johnson was made up of a very complete flying part with a long straight wing with a nacelle at the centre of gravity to house the engine, propeller and additional wheel. The flying element was bolted onto the back of a three-wheel car with two driven wheels at the front. In 1938 Johnson's patent application included a very complete 18-page dossier of drawings and explanations. Several versions of the Autoplane were described in an accompanying file, some being equipped with twin concentric propellers placed either at the front or at the rear.

The war over, the various inventors – T.P. Hall leading the way – could again devote themselves to their researches. These continued to be based around the two systems – integrated and modular – but the concept of modularity came little by little to seem the more realistic and thus the more forward-looking of the two approaches.

The flying car goes to war

In 1932 J. Walter Christie, the famed designer of US Army tanks, proposed a flying version of one of his machines. Equipped with eight wheels, the tank of the air was intended to be capable of reaching 90mph on the ground in order to be able to take off. After having over-flown the enemy lines and landed behind them, it would shed its wings. There were probably few regrets that this project never came to fruition. Christie did come up with a more attractive proposition, however: equipping buses with removable wings. After having taken their passengers on board in the town centre the buses would drive normally to the nearest airport. Once the flying elements had been bolted in place, it was up and away...

In the 1940s the Russians came back to the idea of a flying tank with the Antonov KT, also known as the A-40; it was the work of Oleg Konstantinovitch Antonov, who had already designed a series of highly effective cargo gliders. A T60 light tank served as the A-40's fuselage – and as its landing gear, once the tracks had been removed. A bi-plan wing of 15-metre (49ft 2½in) span and a twin-boom tail were fixed on the tank. The resultant assembly was launched in the air by a tow-plane, and intended to be then left to its own devices to land, if possible behind enemy lines, where it could cause merry havoc. According to Soviet sources of dubious credibility one allegedly successful test took place in 1942, after which the project was abandoned. It had been established that the tow-planes had to be so powerful that only big bombers such as the Petlyakov Pe-8 could be used – and the small numbers of these in service were already engaged on more important missions.

At the same time ideas weren't exactly lacking at the design offices of Britain's Airborne Forces Experimental Establishment at Ringway, near Manchester. Proof of this was the Rotabuggy, invented and developed by Raoul Hafner, later to become Chief Designer (Helicopters) at the Bristol Aeroplane Company and ultimately technical director at Westland Aircraft. The Rotabuggy was nothing more than a Jeep equipped with a two-blade rotor of 40ft 8in diameter and a tapering tail fairing with a twin-fin tailplane. It was tested for the first time on 16 November 1943 and judged satisfactory by the military brass, despite initial tests that were more than a little frightening for the pilot, as stability clearly left something to be desired; maximum speed in the air was 70mph. But the arrival of specialised combat gliders capable of carrying vehicles in their hold, such as the Hamilcar, removed any appeal the Rotobuggy might have had and consigned it to the dustbin of good-but-not-so-good ideas. At the same time Raoul Hafner came up with the similar Rotatank, based on a Valentine infantry tank. This time, though, the project never left the drawing board.

Moulton Taylor, inventor of the Aerocar (see Chapter 8) also proposed a hybrid vehicle, the Fleep – or 'Flying Jeep' – in a bid to obtain financial backing from the military. But unlike his civilian flying car, the Fleep remained just an idea on paper. Much later, the Jeep-O-Plane of Alexander Geraci took up Taylor's principle of modularity, the plane section being towed behind the road-going element. The patent was offered to Ford in 2001, but the car-maker did not pursue matters.

Ten years before the Antonov KT, Walter Christie's flying tanks were depicted on the cover of *Modern Mechanics and Inventions* in this artwork by famed illustrator Norman Saunders (vol.VIII, no.3, for July 1932).

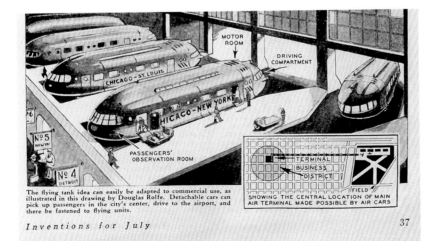

The flying tank idea can easily be adapted to commercial use, as illustrated in this drawing by Douglas Rolfe. Detachable cars can pick up passengers in the city's center, drive to the airport, and there be fastened to flying units.

SHOWING THE CENTRAL LOCATION OF MAIN AIR TERMINAL MADE POSSIBLE BY AIR CARS

*Inventions for July*          37

The idea of a flying tank could easily be adapted for commercial use, with the body of the machine taking the form of a coach – as illustrated in the same issue of *Modern Mechanics and Inventions*.

Traffic in the year 2000, according to a c.1960 drawing by Michel Siméon for Cinzano. The city-dweller uses a 'programmed' chair that moves in three dimensions while avoiding other vehicles. Every home has its blister-garage (right) and there are also parking pods (left). To get to work you could use the 'tube' – a silent underground train operating pneumatically – or sitting or standing travelators. At the top can be seen a supersonic train for travel to neighbouring towns.

**4.**

# A new paradigm: horizontality

In the mid 1940s there was a war-ravaged world to be rebuilt. In the new Atomic Age there was to be a headlong plunge into Modernity, as everyone started to dream of happy tomorrows. There was no doubting that innovatory means of transport would contribute largely to making this grandiose vision of the future a reality, leading mankind towards an ever more distant horizon.

## The post-war aeronautic boom

The entry of the United States into the war meant that there was a pause in civil-aviation research, energies instead being directed to activities more vital to the country than developing a flying car. But at the end of the conflict thousands of Navy and Air Force pilots were demobilised, and numbers of them had no wish to keep their feet forever on the ground. Indeed, the demob payments made to each member of the forces, to help his re-assimilation into civilian society, made it not inconceivable that he could now own a personal or family flying-machine.

In the aftermath of the war several studies of the social and economic evolution of the country came up with figures that were at the very least astonishing: the February 1946 edition of *Air Trails* magazine for example announced that the American administration estimated that 400,000 private planes would be in use by 1955. These predictions were taken seriously, at a very high level. Consequently in the first versions of the 1944 Highway Construction Act members of Congress demanded that airstrips henceforth be constructed alongside the principal highways. Real life seemed to confirm this heady optimism: in 1946 thousands of private planes were sold. You could even buy them in the poshest New York department stores, just like any other consumer durable.

## A new expression of modernity

Specialist aeronautical, automobile, town-planning and DIY magazines, as well as the biggest generalist magazines, started to publish long articles about 'Tomorrow's World' for readers avid to know what the future held. The stories were of unimpeachable optimism and accompanied by extraordinary illustrations – because these articles were above all about their illustrations, and the illustrators gave their imagination free rein. Adding to this, by the beginning of the 1950s the passionate love affair between the US male and his motor car was gathering pace.

Thus, after fifteen years of uncertainty, from the 1929 Wall Street Crash until the end of the Second World War, American society had rediscovered its confidence in the future – and the flying car was one of the most obvious symbols of that wide-open future, in the same way as the 1939 World's Fair in New York or, a few years later, on the old Continent, the Brussels Atomium monument, built for Expo '58, the Brussels World's Fair of 1958.

There was no reason to doubt that all highways would soon conform to the visions of these magazine illustrators: alongside, at regular intervals, would be landing strips where Mr Everyman's family, returning from a weekend at the other end of the country, could land his flying car, fold back its wings, and smoothly merge into the traffic flow to reach his bungalow in the suburbs – or else take a rest with an ice-cold Dr

The celebrated designer Norman Bel Geddes designed the General Motors Futurama pavilion for the 1939 World's Fair in New York. The Futurama showed the world in 1960 in the form of a gigantic diorama. Cars and motorways evidently dominate; there are relatively few skyscrapers, however, as town-planning was principally developing according to a horizontal model.

The extension of urban territory: two-level motorways, rivers as highways, and flying cars. Such would be 'Life in the year 2000' according to *Science et Vie* magazine for May 1959 (no.500).

A vision of a futurist town of the 25th century, in an illustration for *Les Pionniers de la Planète Mars*, a novel by Pierre Ménard: an air-train in the form of an articulated snake and a pot-bellied astrobus with ailerons and fins (*Francs-Jeux*, c.1950).

Pepper's, while a friendly pump attendant filled the tank and cleaned the windscreen before he took to the air again.

It all seemed so simple – so obvious – that few people asked themselves about the negative effects of such an evolution in private transport. For example, nobody seemed frightened by the idea of hundreds of thousands of amateur pilots cluttering up the rush-hour sky above these mega-cities. Yet airborne roadhogs – 'airhogs' perhaps? – freed from the need to keep to demarcated lanes, would no doubt have been even more dangerous than bad drivers with their four wheels firmly on the ground...

*What will the city of tomorrow be like? Here is the giant plastic, metal, and unbreakable glass city of the 21st century. A city of science, of atomic power, of space travel, and of high culture.*

Amazing Stories, *April 1942.*

'Today's research for tomorrow's progress' reads this advertisement for the research centres of Australian car-parts giant Repco Ltd in the 14 October 1959 issue of *Australia To-Day*. Futurist cars and flying saucers make for a classic 1950s image of the future.

TODAY'S RESEARCH
FOR TOMORROW'S PROGRESS

*A section of one of the Repco Research centres.*

The exacting demands of today's motorists necessitate continuous research for tomorrow's development. Repco, the largest manufacturer of Automotive Parts in the Southern Hemisphere, supplies yet one more service to the Australian Automotive Industry — constant skilled research.

**REPCO Limited**   HEAD OFFICE: 618 ELIZABETH STREET, MELBOURNE, AUSTRALIA
AGENTS THROUGHOUT THE WORLD
5630

A city interlaced with motorways but at the same time with flying cars up in the air – such visions were almost a cliché when it came to representing brave new future worlds, as here in French comic *Mandrake* (no.227, 28 August 1969).

The General Motors Rocatomic on the cover of *Science et Techniques pour Tous* (no.14, December 1947): 'powered by atomic energy, this vehicle has no wheels and hovers a few centimetres above the road'.

Private plane, wheel-less car and roads reaching upwards into the sky: verticality remained a feature of the traditional vision of a city of the future as depicted in *Astrotomic* no.28, from 1961.

Whether extraterrestial or under the sea, any self-respecting high-tech city had to be built to a great height in the science-fiction of pre-war days – here in an illustration by Wesso for the cover of the November 1937 *Astounding Stories* (vol 20, no.3).

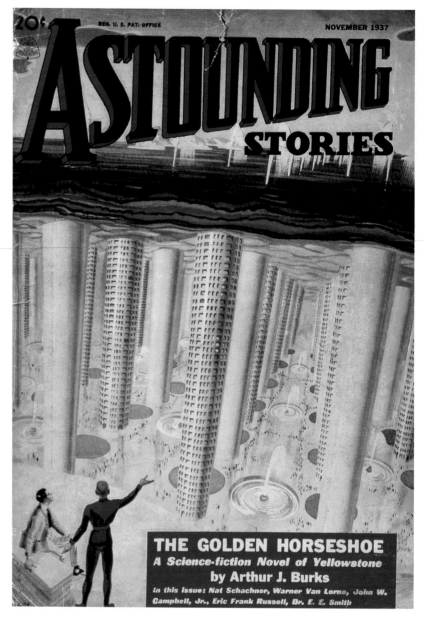

A single-seater air vehicle in flight over the town of tomorrow on the cover of another 1961 copy of *Astrotomic*.

A helicopter in each garage was the theme of this February 1951 cover for *Popular Mechanics*, which represented the Hiller Hornet, 'a personal flying car, sold at 5000 dollars' and powered by turbines situated at the end of the rotors. Supposedly good for 85mph, the Hornet was a still-born project conceived by Hiller Helicopters, of Palo Alto in California, a company that would some years later announce its Aerial Sedan (see Chapter 10).

In his film *Metropolis* (1927), Fritz Lang depicted the city of the future as completely vertical. The different levels corresponded to the social standing of its inhabitants. The exploited workers laboured in basements, while the managing classes lived up high in the buildings, far from the tumult of the machines.

*While fantastic in the extreme today, the airmobile is no more fantastic that the automobile was in the early reign of Queen Victoria. (...)*

*In the future – perhaps sooner than we realize – the problem of gravitation that chains us to the planet will have been solved. (...) This does not mean, in the favorite science-fiction jargon, that we are going to 'neutralize' gravitation, or 'nulify' it. You cannot do away with gravitation, but it will be possible to counteract it. (...) The aircar lifts and rises vertically, first slowly, then faster till you reach the proper legal height for the air lane you wish to travel on. At the correct elevation, you turn on the horizontal flight power. (...) There will be many aerial lanes, for local traffic, express, and long distance. Speeds will be controlled as with land traffic today. Traffic centers will keep you informed on traffic density at all times via radio, so that you will not enter or travel in congested air lanes.(...) At the end of our outing, we descend to the street, garage, or parking lot, simply by reversing the ascending operation, that is, decreasing the counter gravitational field. Soon we contact the earth once more.*

*Hugo Gernsback, Future transportation forecast, December 1956.*

A 'gyroscopic atomic-powered' flying car, as envisaged by one of the greatest artists of the golden age of science-fiction, Frank R. Paul. The illustration was commissioned in 1956 by publisher Hugo Gernsback, originator of the term 'scientifiction', to accompany his article on anti-gravity cars.

## From verticality to horizontality

If the fear of having flying cars taking over town centres was never spelt out, this was perhaps because it was largely not relevant. The futurist visions of the twenties and thirties had been constructed around towns-capes that were above all vertical. In cinema the best example is furnished by the sets for Fritz Lang's film *Metropolis*. In print, the covers and illustrations by Frank R. Paul for the first American pulp science-fiction stories stand out – in particular those published between 1926 and 1929 by Hugo Gernsback's Stellar Publications, such as *Amazing Stories*, *Air Wonder Stories* or *Science Wonder Stories*. Across the Atlantic, similar futurist fare was dished out by Frenchman Henri Lanos in the magazine *Lectures pour Tous*.

In the real world the reference for this school of aesthetics was of course Manhattan. With its island site perforce giving it a finite area, the architecture of the heart of New York could only develop skywards. A communal verticality was the only solution – one that demanded a certain sense of order. Leaning on this concrete example, the city of the future was seen as geometrically perfect and as developing by layer being added to layer, in the manner of a bee hive. Such a future Metropolis could only be a society of insects, ruled over by engineers – a truly mechanistic view of the universe.

In this context, the autogyro seemed the perfect vehicle: its helicopter derivation allowed it to hover over access 'wells' until it could join the traffic flow as either a car or a plane, depending on the nature of the 'road' and whether this was a track suspended in the air or a more 'virtual' trajectory.

But the end of the thirties brought with it a radically different aesthetic: verticality gave way to a vision of the world that was henceforth horizontal. City centres dominated by skyscrapers stayed as they were, but alongside them the dreams of the average American had moved out to the suburbs. Here he imagined a world where a pleasant house had a garage to one side (with space – why not? – for his flying car), a patch of lawn at the front, and a small garden at the rear. All of this was neat and tidy, because the Land of the Free was above all about order, whether vertical or horizontal.

The flying car in the end was therefore conceived not to initiate new levels of traffic or to aid access to the buildings of cities made up of skyscrapers, but rather to facilitate a rational occupation of an ever-growing territory. It was a vehicle intended to allow the honest citizen to travel as rapidly as possible between his place of work, an office in town, and his place of residence, a bungalow in the suburbs.

In the pre-war years the American dream was in essence a popular and largely collective vision of the 'nation'. The period that followed, in contrast, saw the advance of a spirit of individualism. In this context a hybrid vehicle seemed the ideal instrument to help reposition the individual and his family unit in this brave new world.

Arthur C. Radebaugh created this 'Drive-Up Hotel' in 1948 and re-worked it in 1958 for his weekly cartoon strip *Closer Than We Think*. Visitors land on the roof before going to sunbathe on the beach or taking to the road (in the same vehicle in which they arrived)...

In 1946 Theodore P. Hall came up with the Hall Flying
Car, subsequently renamed the Convair Model 116.

**5.**

## Theodore P. Hall and the Golden Age of modular machines

In the immediate post-war years Theodore P. Hall continued his work on modularity, which he had pioneered with his Roadable Airplane of 1939. The principle became the touchstone for most of the inventors in this domain, whether simple amateurs trying to bring their dreams to life in their garage at home or those aero-industry professionals who had started to lay down more sophisticated projects.

### The Hall Flying Car

At the end of the Second World War, Theodore P. Hall resigned from the Consolidated Vultee Aircraft Corporation (which had become Convair in 1943), so as to devote himself entirely to the project for a flying car that had begun with the Roadable Airplane (see Chapter 3). This was a time of euphoria and idealism. Soon he was joined by Tommy Thompson, who was both a friend and a former colleague. Together they set up a small business and took on a handful of workers to build a new Roadable Airplane prototype, soon re-named the HFC – or Hall Flying Car.

The aircraft part of the HFC featured a 90bhp Franklin engine operating a two-blade wooden propeller and the car element was powered by a 26.5bhp Crosley engine – in fact the fuselage was similar in shape to a Crosley mini-car, although the HFC was only a three-wheeler and closer in size to a Volkswagen Beetle.

Working conditions were crude: the aluminium sheet for the body panels was cut by hand and beaten into shape over lengths of steel tubing, using a rubber mallet. But by the beginning of 1946, Theodore Hall and Tom Faulconer were able to start initial testing of the HFC, and this proved most encouraging.

### A diversion down south: the SAC Aerocar

Whilst Theodore Hall and his small team were perfecting their machine, they were approached by the Southern Aircraft Corporation, the aeronautical division of the Portable Products Corporation, an important concern in Garland, Texas. Hall's researches interested the Texans, and a deal was rapidly concluded. Hall moved to Garland for a time and oversaw the construction of what became the SAC Aerocar.

Again there was a three-wheel car forming the fuselage, but this time with the single wheel at the front. The flat-six air-cooled Franklin engine developed 130bhp and powered a front-mounted propeller, and the removable fabric-covered aircraft element comprised a wing with a span of 30ft and two booms carrying the tailplane and twin tailfins. The end result had a glider-like look and the car part was particularly elegant. In flight, with the drive to the rear wheels disconnected, steering was by a second set of pedals, with the steering wheel serving as the joy-stick.

Most of the test flights were undertaken by a test pilot by the name of C.T. Prescott, from the Major's Field airport in Greenville, Texas. Despite slightly better performance than the Hall Flying Car – maximum speed 168mph, cruising speed 110mph and a range of a roughly 310 miles – the SAC Aerocar was deemed insufficiently powerful, and never made it to production. In any case, the boss of Southern Aircraft regarded it as nothing more than an experiment.

The SAC Aerocar (NX 59711) in flight, in 1946: the machine was capable of over 125mph.

The Southern Aircraft Corporation's Aerocar, conceived by Theodore P. Hall, was on the cover of the February 1947 issue of *Science et Vie*, which featured several projects for flying cars then under study.

After numerous successful flights, the Convair 116 was deemed technically satisfactory, but aesthetically it left something to be desired. The Convair company soon decided to start a new project.

Theodore P. Hall, on the left, working on the design of one of his famed road-going planes, in the mid 1940s.

## The Convair 116

Meanwhile the HFC prototype cobbled together by Hall had attracted the attention of the team running Convair. They were totally convinced that the US was going to enter a period of very strong growth and that the aero industry in particular was going to be at the heart of this boom. To respond to the envisaged demand the firm felt it urgent to develop a plane that was lightweight, economical and easy to fly – with, if possible, the bonus of a little touch of modernity – and in 1945 has already built the Convair 111, a small private plane intended to be affordable for the man in the street. As a further impetus to this train of thought, Convair had an engineer on its staff with a keen interest in flying cars. This was William B. Stout, who had already worked with Waldo Waterman (see Chapter 2) and with George Spratt on the Convair 103 (see Chapter 1).

The consequence of all this was that Theordore Hall's former employers bought up HFC, and transferred its operations from the suburbs of Dallas to the main Convair factory at Lindbergh Field, near San Diego. The HFC was re-named the Convair Model 116 and the prototype given the registration NX90654.

For its first flight, on 12 July 1946, it was piloted by Russell R. Rogers, a Convair engineer working on the project. With effect from the third flight, Rogers was replaced by another pilot, Bill Martin. The series of test-flights was satisfactory but the machine was felt to need more power, so in August the 90bhp Franklin engine was replaced by a 95bhp unit. By the end of the year the Model 116 had racked up 66 successful flights and the decision was taken to build a more spacious and better-performing version which would be more saleable.

## A flying saloon car: the ConvAirCar

Some important modifications were carried out to Hall's initial design. Henceforth the automotive element would be a proper motor car – a normal four-seat saloon. In looks the Model 118 consequently ended up as one of the most attractive flying cars, and for good reason: it owed a great deal to Henry Dreyfuss. A pupil of Norman Bel Geddes, Dreyfuss was one of the most respected industrial designers of the time, and his portfolio included telephones for Bell, tractors for John Deere, thermostats for Honeywell and cameras for Polaroid.

Good looks were in any case a key requirement laid down by the directors of Convair, who felt this vital for the success of the project. William Wold, the sales director, consequently asked for several proposals from another talented automotive designer, Tucker Madawick. At the time Madawick lived in London, where he was responsible for the European office of one of the century's most important industrial designers, Raymond Loewy. Madawick would later be called upon to work on the controversial Tucker car, before taking charge of the design department of Radio Corporation of America, better known as RCA.

In order to reduce the weight of the car part of the Model 118, which was still powered by a 26.5bhp Crosley engine, the body was made of glassfibre-reinforced plastic (grp), which was lighter and stronger than metal. This was a genuine innovation, as it would only be some years later that glassfibre would start to be used by the motor industry – notably by Chevrolet, for its Corvette. The weight of the automotive element of Hall's machine, a very reasonable 7cwt, meant that a modest fuel consumption was claimed. The aircraft part was composed of a pair of wings with a 34ft 6in span, a cruciform tail assembly, a second fuel tank, and a 190bhp Lycoming radial engine powering a front-mounted three-blade Sensenich propeller.

The process of uniting the two modules was ingeniously simple. The car was reversed under the plane section, which was supported on a lightweight three-point undercarriage, and then an assembly containing the cockpit controls was lowered through the car roof into the driving compartment, in front of the dashboard, so that the driver became the pilot without having to change seat. The tripod undercarriage was then folded, and the machine could take off for its destination airport where

The Convair Model 111 (NX90652) was a small plane for two people sitting side by side. Initially it was thought of as being a 'roadable aircraft'. However, from the outset of testing in 1945 the engine's cooling system proved deficient, and the machine received no further development.

*What I have in mind is a UNIVERSAL VEHICLE – an idea which goes beyond what our imagination has been capable of achieving up until now.*

*William B. Stout, 1948.*

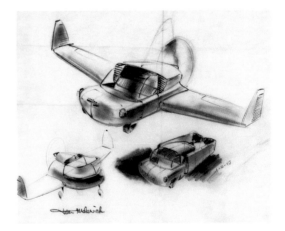

An all-in-one system with wings that fold back against the sides, drawn up for Convair in 1948 by industrial designer Tucker Madawick. At the same time Ted Hall's ConvAirCar was being successfully tested.

The plane part of the ConvAirCar 118 was intended to be left at the airport, the happy owner of the road-going element renting it out as required.

Convair used a bit of glamour to promote its Model 118
(aka ConvAirCar): here, in the twinkle of an eye, the
two modules have been joined together. The young
ladies are evidently impressed...

Theodore Hall's ConvAirCar was more than just a
real car with elegant styling: it was arguably the very
image of what a flying car should be, as here in the
Californian skies...

it would duly shed its 'flight module'. An alternative configuration was also considered. William Chana, a Convair engineer, proposed doing away with the entire tail unit and instead fixing a spar carrying a second wing, of vee-section, to the front of the module. No testing was carried out to see if the idea worked or not.

The first example of the Model 118 carried the registration NX90850 and was successfully tested on 15 November 1947 by a new test-pilot, Reuben P. Snodgrass, still accompanied by Lawrence Phillips. The performance was most satisfactory: the cruising speed in the air was 130mph, while on the road the Convair 118 managed 70mph.

Two days later, the news made the front page of the *New York Times*: a flying car had been in the air over San Diego for a total of one hour and 18 minutes!

The directors of Convair had been present for this memorable test flight. There was general enthusiasm. The sales department predicted minimum sales of 160,000, based on a catalogue price of only $1500 – this without the aircraft 'module'. The idea was to keep the price down to that of a regular saloon car by renting out the aircraft element via a network of franchised agents at every aerodrome, rather than selling it outright.

Convair had just taken over the Stinson Aircraft Company, a respected aircraft builder, and the firm was going to be given the task of making and selling the new machine. A team of sales reps was soon expected to be covering the country trumpeting the merits of the wonder machine, redubbed the Stinson Aircar and ultimately the ConvAirCar.

Alas, on 18 November, while on a routine flight, the prototype ran out of fuel on the approach to Lindbergh Field and crashed into the desert, near Chula Vista. The aircraft module wasn't damaged but the car part was completely destroyed and the pilot wounded. Reuben Snodgrass later admitted that he had mistaken the car petrol gauge for that of the aircraft module...

The test flights of the Model 118 began again on 29 January 1948, undertaken by Bill Martin and W.G. Griswold, using a new prototype again registered NX90850 and comprising the old aircraft module and a new car fuselage, the fifth built since the acquisition of the HFC. The Model 118 proved perfectly reliable, even if certain problems remained, such as a poor power-to-weight ratio.

The mood was still one of optimism, Convair speaking of mass-production, of a military version, and even of a more powerful family model having a flying module with a 42ft 6in wingspan. In other words the project was still being talked up. Unfortunately the November crash had had a disastrous effect on many potential purchasers – and this at a time when the market was awash with thousands of small planes

The cockpit of the ConvAirCar, as depicted in Convair's 1948 prospectus: the aircraft controls were inserted into the cabin through the opening roof and positioned in front of the steering wheel. The pilot/driver retained the same seat.

Aero Willys, the car of the future: in this c.1952 catalogue Willys presented its new model by alluding to the world of aviation, doubtless to play up the supposedly aerodynamic design of the car.

*The flying car dropped swiftly in an obscure part of the city.*

*Issac Asimov,* Evidence, *in* Astounding Science Fiction vol.38 no.1 *(September 1946).*

A police officer electrocutes a criminal in front of a flying car similar to the ConvAirCar in the German edition of a story by Sam Merwin Jr (Terra Nova, 1968).

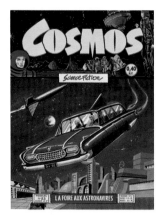

The function is different but the design is similar to Ted Hall's machines in the case of this space saloon depicted on the cover of a 1961 *Cosmos* comic.

built towards the end of the war, duly disarmed and for sale at a low price. Above all, it had to be admitted that the economic climate had markedly deteriorated. The dream of a society where everyone could afford a flying car of their own was rapidly vanishing: sales of personal aeroplanes for 1948 were only a quarter of those for 1946 – and projected sales for 1949 were even lower.

When it became evident that the post-war boom would be a long time coming, Convair abandoned the project – in which it had nonetheless invested more than $800,000 – and handed Theodore Hall all stock and materials as well as the prototypes, as provided for in his contract, should the company withdraw from the venture.

Hall duly founded the T.P. Hall Engineering Corporation, in San Diego, to carry the project forward. The aero-car changed its name yet again, to become the Hall Flying Automobile. Commercially, therefore, the Hall Flying Car was back to square one – only with the benefit of a certain technical evolution, because of the progress in various areas that had been achieved in moving from the HPC to the Model 118. Meanwhile, Hall tried to sell the glassfibre car module on its own, for the modest price of $500-700, under the Airway name.

But without serious financial backing and the support of a company to build the vehicle and promote the project, the enterprise was doomed. Theodore Hall was a professional engineer, and the making of flying cars was no out-of-hours hobby for him, but a passion that had to achieve financial viability in order to survive. Without this, there was nothing left but for him to throw in the towel.

A few years later Theodore P. Hall retired and settled in New York – leaving his various flying cars to deteriorate in a hangar in El Cajon, in southern California. Only the 1939 Roadable Aircraft was rescued in good condition, but it was destroyed in 1978, in the fire at the San Diego Aerospace Museum, where it was on show. Hall's archives, however, are still at the museum: these documents are an important source of information for anyone interested in flying vehicles, and allow Hall his rightful place of honour in the tormented history of this field of activity.

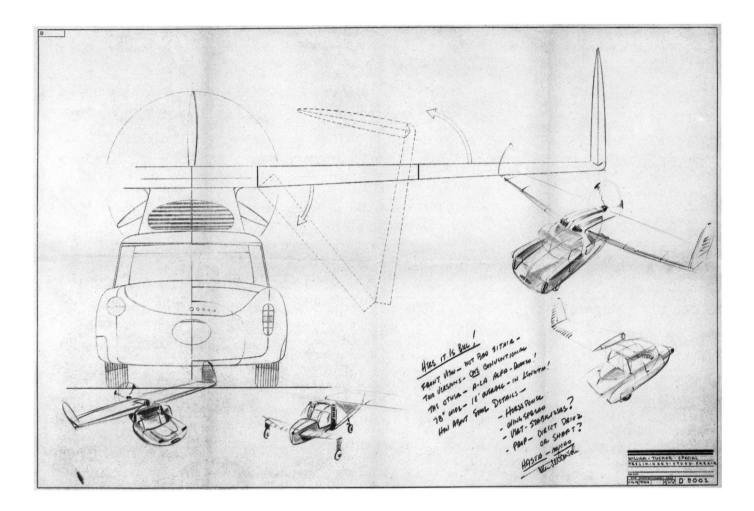

Tucker Madawick thought up a system of folding wings for a vehicle he named the William Tucker Special or the Carair – but in the note that accompanies this preliminary artwork he asks Bill Wold, sales chief of Convair, for additional information.

The flying car as a publicity image, here for Texaco in 1947. A number of such machines, from the Arrowbile to the various projects of T.P. Hall, used normal petrol.

Robert E. Fulton's Airphibian FA-2 in flight. It was
the first flying car certified for production by the
US administration.

**6.**

# Robert E. Fulton and his Airphibian:
# within a whisker of success

The machine on which Robert Edison Fulton Jr set to work in the immediate post-war years combined something of the commercial-mindedness of the Convair and the more home-built character of Waldo Waterman's efforts. This doubtless owes to Fulton being both an unrepentant dreamer and a visionary inventor.

## An inventor of genius

Robert Edison Fulton Jr was a sort of Jack-of-all-Trades who was as brilliant as he was versatile. No doubt this was as much due to his middle name as his family background, one of his great-grandfathers being the inventor of the steam-boat.

Above all, he seemed incapable of staying in any one place for long. After a secondary education in Geneva – where he built a car from motorcycle parts and a $1/3$hp engine – he went home to the United States to go up to Harvard, as a stepping-stone to returning to Europe. This he duly did, spending time in Paris before fetching up at the University of Vienna, where he gained a degree in architecture in 1932, at the age of 23.

He then decided to return to the States, stopping off in London. There, in the course of a meal, he announced to his hosts – to impress a young lady amongst the guests – that he was going to do a round-the-world trip by motorcycle. Committed to this somewhat crazy project, in 1933 he travelled from England to Tokyo on a Douglas flat-twin, via Europe, North Africa, the Indies, Malaysia and China, with just a few sea crossings breaking up the mileage. From the expedition Fulton brought back nearly 40,000 feet of film and several books of notes and drawings. The film that was created from this material was shown at a series of conferences, further promoted by Fulton's book *One-Man Caravan*.

Having returned home, Robert Fulton married, learnt to fly a plane, and became an aerial photographer for Pan American World Airways. One day he climbed to the top of the Empire State Building and took a sequence of forty photos which once pieced together offered a 360-degree panorama of the New York horizon, something nobody had thought of doing before. But Robert Fulton was that kind of person...

By this time the US was on the point of joining the Second World War. Fulton developed the Gunairstructor pilot-training system, a flight-and-combat simulator, and put it into production. In 1942 the Navy ordered 500 of the machines, to a value of six million dollars.

## The birth of the Airphibian

In the course of the training he provided for users of the Gunairstructor, Fulton often used private planes to get to military air-bases. He came to realise how much time was lost getting to and from the aerodromes, as well as the additional cost of having to hire a car. He soon had the idea of a hybrid machine, one that was both plane and car at the same time, and would be easy to convert and use. It has to be said that in the Fulton family the transport bug was handed down from generation to generation – one of his ancestors founded the Greyhound bus company and his father ran Mack Trucks, an important US builder of lorries.

At the end of the war Robert Fulton's company, the Flight Training Research Association Inc, could boast a well-equipped plant and highly qualified staff, but could no longer count on an assured income. Fulton therefore decided to create Continental Inc, specifically to build a flying car, and he duly set up a new workshop in Newtown, Connecticut.

Assisted by his chief mechanic, Wayne Dasher, he set about developing a machine he called the Airphibian. Whether he was just being exaggeratedly discreet or was merely a touch paranoid, Fulton took pains not to attract the attention of other plane manufacturers. The prototype, designated simply under the code 'Invention No.2', was developed in secret, with highway testing taking place at night on the deserted roads around Danbury, and with the first test flights before the end of 1945.

With test pilot Frazer Dougherty at the controls, Airphibian 1 was shown to the press on 7 November 1946, and received a warm welcome;

The flying car proved just the thing for escaping when pursued by cavemen. A cover for *Earthman, Go Home!* by Poul Anderson (Ace D-479, 1960).

Only seven minutes to make the transformation from plane to car: the Airphibian of Robert E. Fulton fascinated not only the US media but also the European press, as witnessed by this full-page report in *The Illustrated London News* for 23 November 1946.

The first version of the Airphibian (NX60374) during
a presentation to the press in 1946. The car and plane
parts of the machine are ready to be united for the
benefit of the Universal Newsreel cameras.

indeed, the media would continue to support the venture. For example, in 1948 they followed Mr and Mrs Fulton from Connecticut to New York when they went to see popular musical *Kiss me Kate!* on Broadway. This expedition was the subject of a photo-story in *Life* magazine, just one of countless articles on the Airphibian to appear in the frontline press of the day.

## A first – certification by the US federal administration

After a hundred hours of flight in the first prototype, an operational Airphibian II was built, registered N74104. It benefited from various improvements, notably to the foot controls. Tested in flight for the first time on 21 May 1947, it was submitted for examination by the CAA – the Civil Aeronautics Administration, later to become the Federal Aviation Administration, or FAA – with the aim of obtaining the necessary authorisation to begin production.

Like the machines of Theodore Hall, the Airphibian was a completely modular vehicle, but of a largely different design. The car element was a small two-seater using four aircraft landing wheels housed in sponsons, while the aircraft part was constituted by an add-on fuselage with a one-piece wing and a single-fin tailplane. The fundamental principle remained the same, however: between uses the flying element remained at the airport. Disconnecting this tail section, which was extremely light, was a one-man job, and all that then remained was to remove the three-blade prop from the front of the car. It was claimed that four minutes sufficed to remove the aircraft elements and seven minutes to put them back in place. Furthermore, a safety system meant that it was impossible to start the vehicle if everything hadn't been properly fixed.

The Airphibian's shortcomings were those shared by all the flying-car prototypes, as a result of the need to keep weight down: the cockpit was cramped and not particularly comfortable and the aluminium body wasn't very robust. The engine, an air-cooled four-cylinder, gave a top speed in the air of 110mph and the 30-gallon tank translated into a respectable range of approximately 350 miles. On the road, though, the Airphibian's performance wasn't as good as that of the ConvAirCar, its principal rival, as it could barely manage 50mph.

By the beginning of 1950 Fulton had a flight of three Airphibians under his command and between them they had covered over 200,000 miles and undergone 6000 coupling and uncoupling operations. The four-cylinder engine had been replaced by a 150bhp 'six' and thanks to this increase in power the Airphibian II could now break the 50mph barrier on the road and manage 120mph in flight. At the end of May some minor modifications were made to bring the machine into total

*We went up by a route I had not known about and ended up on the Northside launching platform, high above New Brooklyn and overlooking Manhattan Crater. I drove while the Old Man talked. Once we were out of local control he told me to set it automatic on Des Moines, Iowa. (...) I roaded the car about five miles this side of Grinnell and we started looking for the McLain farm (...). Shortly the road was parked both sides with duos and groundcars and triphibs. (...) But we didn't get there. First it was a bridge out and I didn't have room enough to make the car hop it, quite aside from the small matter of traffic regulations for a duo on the ground. We circled to the south and came in again, the only remaining route. (...) The Old Man vetoed taking to the air and making a pass over the triangulated spot. He said it was useless. We headed for Des Moines. Instead of parking at the toll gates we paid to take the car into the city proper.*

Robert Heinlein, The Puppet Masters, *1951.*

Madam, what could be more simple than to do your shopping by Airphibian FA-2? After having flown from your garden suburb, all you have to is spend a few minutes with an adjustable spanner and then you can take to the road to reach your favourite grocer...

The Airphibian in its second incarnation, the FA-2
(registered N74104): after having separated the
two parts of the machine, it was straightforward to
stow the prop on the side of the fuselage, under the
admiring gaze of the family.

conformity with the law, and on 21 December 1950 Fulton was finally given all the legal clearances by the federal aviation authorities. This certification was a first for a flying car, and meant that the Airphibian could now officially enter its production phase.

The first production model of the Airphibian II, vehicle number FA-2-101, left the Fulton works carrying registration N74153. It was soon followed by a prototype Airphibian III with a cantilever wing, this being certified by the CAA in June 1952. The first production example of this model, vehicle number FA-3-101, was registered N74154. So by 1952 the winds looked set fair for the Airphibian.

AVIATION

FIRST ROADABLE PLANE APPROVED BY CIVIL AERONAUTICS ADMINISTRATION IS FULTON AIRPHIBIAN (ABOVE). FLYING VERSION IS IN AIR, CAR VERSION ON RUNWAY

# AIR INVENTIONS

Light-plane industry hopes they will pull it out of a tailspin

Since the war more than 50,000 Americans tried owning and flying their own airplanes. Many of them have quickly become discouraged, sold their planes and reduced their flying to occasional weekend jaunts in rented planes. This slump in what was hoped would be a postwar boom stems from three things: 1) it is inconvenient to use private planes; 2) they are too expensive; 3) people are afraid of accidents. To combat these problems

and save itself from bankruptcy the light-plane industry has come up with a variety of new developments, such as a plane which can be used in the air and on the highway, a low-priced plane (*next page*) and devices which make landings easier and safer (*p. 142*). Taken together these developments should enable more and more people to do as Marjorie Harrison (*p. 144*) has done—own and regularly fly a personal plane on a salary of $62 a week.

AIRPHIBIAN CAN BE CONVERTED FROM CAR TO PLANE IN FIVE MINUTES. CAR BACKS INTO THE FUSELAGE, PROPELLER FASTENS TO NOSE. PRICE IS STILL A SECRET

*Life* magazine showed a close interest in the Airphibian in the context of an article on the future of private flying in its 25 October 1948 issue.

### A success that proved fatal

Eight FA-3s were placed on firm order by the US government, for use by CAA inspectors, and at the same time private individuals registered their interest and even proposed to pay in advance, at a premium, in order to have the first examples on sale. The Airphibian wasn't cheap: originally estimated as costing $5000, its price rose first to $7000 and then to $10,000. Certain improvements were envisaged, such as the use of a new and lighter Sensenich propeller with four blades instead of three and a smaller diameter, thereby lowering the centre of gravity of the car part of the machine, and consequently improving its behaviour on the road.

The eight FA-3s were duly built, but some of Robert Fulton's partners had become tired of waiting: the certification procedure had been long and very expensive, and the money men reckoned that that they weren't getting a sufficient return on their investment. So they cut off funds to Fulton and when they left they took with them some of the completed planes – a move which prevented the first commercial deliveries from taking place.

Ironically, then, the very success of the machine caused its failure. Having seen the potential of the Airphibian after its certification, and already imagining an American sky filled with flying cars in the very near future, the investors tried on their own behalf to interest big US companies such as General Motors in taking up the machine. But without Fulton on board, their attempts were doomed.

Knocked sideways, Robert E. Fulton was forced to sell his invention to aircraft-maker Taylorcraft, in a bid to give it a second chance. But he was on a hiding to nothing. Not particularly inclined to see this strange machine in competition with its own planes, one imagines, the company lost no time in burying the project.

Today an example of the Airphibian, number N74154, belongs to the Smithsonian National Air and Space Museum in Washington and was recently on show in the Canadian Aviation and Space Museum in Ottawa.

As for Robert Edison Fulton Jr, he carried on as an inventor – leaving behind something in the order of 70 patents. Amongst other things, during the Cold War he developed the Skyhook, a means of helping spies escape from enemy territory that was popularised in the final scene of the 1965 James Bond film *Thunderball*. Consisting of a jumpsuit attached to a helium balloon, it allowed its user to make a quick airborne escape before being picked up by an aircraft.

Dying in 2004 at the age of 95, Robert Fulton was also a sculptor, photographer and poet. His son, Robert Fulton III, who took over the family workshop with a view to perhaps relaunching the Airphibian, had time to do no more than restore one of the prototypes before dying when he crashed his Cessna in 2002.

In the short history of the flying car, never had the idea come so close to succeeding as with the Airphibian.

The road-going part of the Airphibian on the highway, in a cover image from *Science et Voyages* (issue no.18 of May 1947).

A bizarre vehicle for the mad scientist, the young hero and his dog: an illustration by H. Schaffner for *Les aventures du Docteur Boldos en Lugarie* by Arthur Allan (Michel Roland, 1950).

A scene from the 1968 Ken Hughes film *Chitty Chitty Bang Bang*, based on a children's story by James Bond creator Ian Fleming: the flying car created by an eccentric professor is the film's star turn.

**7.**

# In pursuit of the dream

Theodore P. Hall and Robert Fulton weren't alone in trying to bring to life their vision of personal transport in the years that followed the Second World War. In the wake of these inspired inventors followed a number of individuals, in the United States but equally in Europe, who tried – quite often with some difficulty – to live their dream, just at the moment when post-war enthusiasm for aviation was on the wane.

### Alternative approaches to modularity

In the second half of the 1940s modular machines made the running, these consisting of a road vehicle with a removable aircraft section; this was the format chosen by those constructors who seemed in with a chance of making a working flying car.

### The Boggs Airmaster

Conceived by Herbert D. Boggs and Helen J. Boggs of Omaha, Nebraska, the Boggs Airmaster was the subject of a patent application of April 1944 under the description 'Convertible Air and Land Conveyance'.

In the broad church of the modular movement the Airmaster stood apart. In fact the only part shared between car and plane was the bodywork. This was seen as being fitted either on a 16ft chassis with its own powertrain or to an aircraft understructure with a 38ft wingspan and a tricycle undercarriage incorporating retractable main wheels in the wings and a twin-boom tail. Conversion was claimed to take less than five minutes. With a 145bhp engine and a rear-mounted or 'pusher' propeller, it was envisaged that the cruising speed would be 130mph, for a range of 500 miles.

For this original approach to modularity to work, there would have to have been a network of agents in place at aerodromes around the country, equipped to take in the aircraft modules and to provide everyone arriving by air with a car chassis equipped with the running gear of his choice. The owner would have his own cabin, finished to his tastes, and would hire the flying module and the rolling chassis as and when needed.

Although it received a certain amount of press coverage, the Boggs Airmaster was never built.

### The Travelplane

In 1947 George Hervey of Roscoe, California, unveiled his Travelplane. It comprised a road-going module 16ft long to which a flying part with a 39ft wingspan could be fitted, equipped with a 200bhp Ranger engine offering a claimed cruising speed of 120mph and a range of four hours.

The transformation from air to road took only six minutes, stopwatch in hand – or at least did so when Hervey carried out the demonstration himself. But this was a bit like those hucksters at markets who sell gadgets to slice your vegetables in a trice: try by yourself, in the comfort of your own home, and it's a different matter. The truth would undoubtedly have been that after an hour spent struggling to un-do a

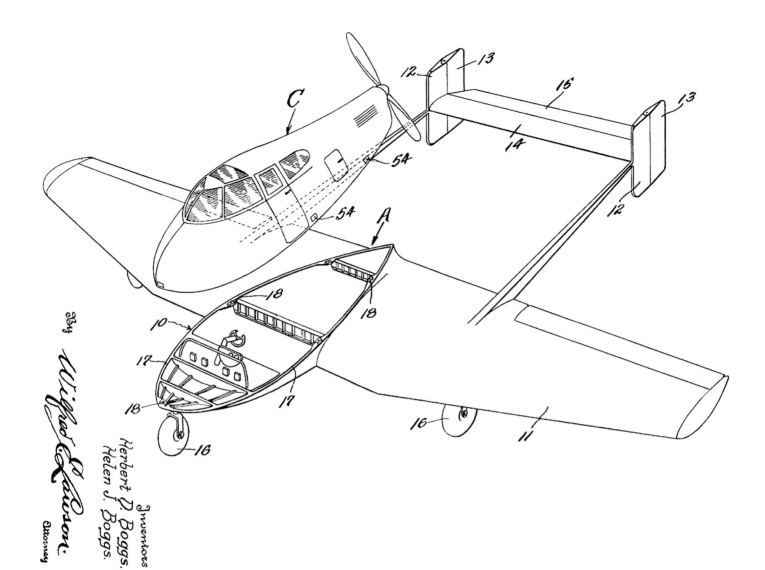

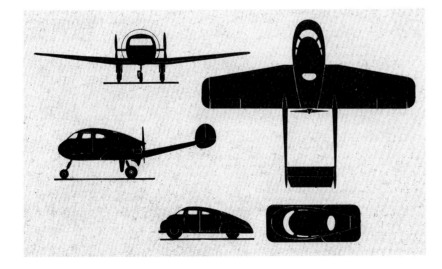

The patent for the modular 'Convertible Air and Land Conveyance' – otherwise known as the Boggs Airmaster – lodged in 1944 by Herbert and Helen Boggs.

In the design for the Boggs Airmaster only the upper half of the fuselage is shared by the aircraft and car elements, as illustrated in this drawing from *Science et Vie* no.353, for February 1947.

wing, the happy owner of a Travelplane would then sweat even more trying to get it into a trailer attached to the car, if he was lucky.

The Travelplane was certain built – but did it ever fly?

**The York Commuter**

The company that pushed the notion of modularity to its extreme limit was perhaps the York Research Corporation of New York, with its York Commuter.

As presented to the media, the machine – which in the end was never built – consisted of a completely independent small car, weighing a somewhat implausible 180kg, which was driven up a ramp into the cabin of a twin-engined aircraft. The controls of the plane could then be operated by the driver of the car without his having to leave his seat.

With a load of one small car and two passengers, the plane was said to be capable of 115mph, with a range of 600 miles, whilst its take-off speed was only 45mph. The aircraft, which had a three-wheel undercarriage, was of course totally self-contained and didn't need the car part in order to function. In fact, is it correct to refer to such a machine as a 'flying car', even if it fulfilled the same role?

**A detour via France: the Aviauto**

France deserves a note in the margins of the early post-war history of the flying car, if only for the efforts of M. de la Fournière, an engineer attached to the Société Nationale de Constructions Aéronautiques du Centre.

After an abortive first attempt involving a car coupled to a twin-engined monoplane – the two machines both having their own power unit and the car serving as the aircraft cockpit – in 1947 he came up with a design that was certainly original.

The basis remained a twin-engined monoplane with a 13.7m (45ft) wingspan and a removable front fuselage – you could literally choose the fuselage that best suited your needs, whether you wanted to transport freight, letters, the injured on a stretcher, or just passengers. One of the fuselages was purely and simply a five-seater car. The aircraft controls, which folded away in the interior of the plane, were designed to drop down into the chosen fuselage – or the car – through an opening roof, the instrument panel being visible through a sequence of mirrors. All the controls for the propellers, the undercarriage and the flaps were located in the wing or in the fuselage, but within easy reach of the pilot's seat, which was the same as the driver's seat in the car. The aircraft part was seen as being equipped with regular landing gear, independent of the car, or with a three-wheel undercarriage of which the front wheel, part of the car's chassis, was able to retract under the car bonnet.

So as not to be just so much dead weight, the car's engine was to

Made to be used in all the elements: *Un Aérodyne sur la Mer* by John Rackham, in its 1966 French edition by Robert Lafont, in the Plein Vent collection. First published in English as *Watch on Peter* (1964).

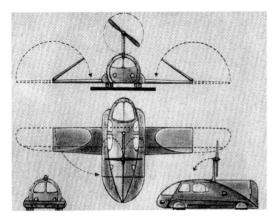

In 1944 a certain K.F. Fonck thought up the AF-P6 flying car, with its two-way folding wings, as shown in these drawings in the August 1956 edition of German magazine *Hobby*.

First seen in 1962, the Hanna-Barbera cartoon strip *The Jetsons* depicted the daily life of an ordinary family in the 21st century. By then everyone travelled by flying car – in fact something closer to a flying saucer, as the wheels have almost disappeared. This is a German version of the strip, dating from 1971.

A scheme for M. de la Fournière's Aviauto, as shown in February 1947's *Science et Vie* (no.353); as with Ted Hall's ConvAirCar, the aircraft controls were envisaged as dropping through the roof of the vehicle.

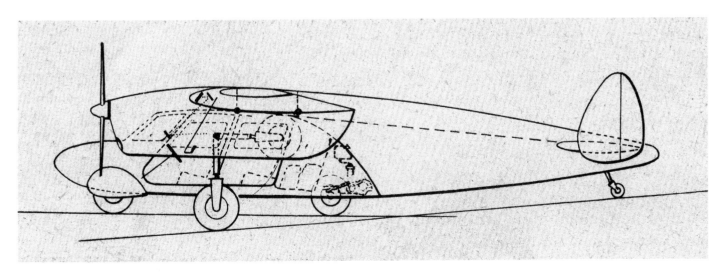

be used in flight as an auxiliary power unit for heating, de-misting, lighting and operating the radio. With its two 200bhp aero-engines the machine was envisaged as achieving up to 200mph when coupled to a normal fuselage. The aerodynamic efficiency claimed for the car was such that in Aviauto mode, in other words with the car as the fuselage, the airborne performance was expected to be only slightly less, with a cruising speed of 165mph.

Back on the ground, the car element, with a weight of 450kg (8.9cwt) and a 32bhp engine, was envisaged as being good for approaching 70mph. It was comparable to a lightweight production saloon in its internal dimensions, comfort and roadholding. There was just one snag: the road-going part of the Aviauto, just like the flying part, never left M. de la Fournière's drawing board...

**Fight-back of the 'all-in-ones'**

Certain projects of the immediate post-war years revived the idea of folding wings: these seemed more in line with public expectations, in terms of ease of use, and were a clear reflection of the fantasy of being able to take to the air anywhere one wanted to, rather than solely from an aerodrome.

In the Federal Republic of Germany in 1962 an engineer working for Helicopter Technik Wagner, Alfred Vogt (not to be confused with science-fiction writer Alfred van Vogt), came up with several designs of helicopter, including a hybrid road-going model, the Rotocar IIII. The project was built and tested, but never got beyond the experimental stage.

The Aérauto of M. Chalaoux, based around a plane with no vertical tailfin and with wings that folded; the artwork is taken from the same issue of French magazine *Science et Vie* as the preceding drawing of the de la Fournière machine.

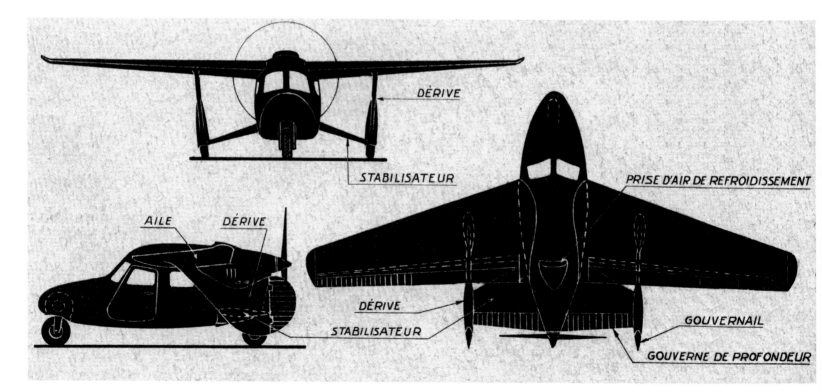

### Return to France: the Chalaoux Aérauto

In France engineer Chalaoux was meanwhile working on the Aérauto, which was announced to the press in 1947. The machine didn't have an orthodox rear section to the fuselage, but merely a stubby twin-fin tail unit. There was a high-set wing with a 9.4m (30ft 10in) span and a tailplane equipped with elevators, all this at the rear of the bodywork/fuselage. Two large vertical fins linked the wings to the tailplane and ended in fairings for the rear wheels, which were not retractable. The Aérauto was supposed to fly like an ordinary plane, despite this unusual configuration. On the ground, steering was by the single front wheel, which in flight lodged inside the machine's nose.

The cabin was only a two-seater, with the seats side-by-side, but it was described as being comfortably fitted-out, with sound-deadened side panels. At the rear the engine bay housed a 140bhp Renault engine, acting directly on the rear-mounted 'pusher' propeller, which was shielded, during road use, by the two tail-fins.

For road use the wings folded towards the rear, in which format the machine had a width of 2.6m (8ft 6in), and a length of 4.5m (14ft 9in), with a height of under 2m (6ft 6in). There was thus no need for any dismantling before the machine took to the road. All this constituted a radically new conception in aviation, but the Aérauto never saw the light of day.

### The Italians: Aernova and Aerauto

In contrast with the Chalaoux project, numerous all-in-one designs of the time were in fact nothing more than ordinary private planes with folding wings, pivoting so that they could be folded rearwards through 90 degrees and either sit outboard of the fuselage or on top of it.

On certain machines the wings were equipped with a more complex folding system that allowed them to fold vertically either side of the fuselage. This bolder technical approach was showcased in the flying cars of Italian engineer Luigi Pellarini.

Italy had already put a flying car in the air in 1945, but it was the creation of a one-man band, commandante Ercolano Ercolani, and the good reception given to his Erco-Spider proved a flash in the pan. Luigi Pellarini, on the other hand, did his best to stack the cards in his favour by setting up Milan-based New York Costruzioni Aeronautiche in 1947, in order to pull in financial backing to develop his first flying-car project.

The Aeronova AER 1 was a three-wheeler with a three-seat all-metal car body with two seats at the front and one behind; the single wheel was at the front and drive went to the rear wheels, all three wheels having hydraulic brakes. A wing with a span of 9.6m (31ft 6in) was attached above the rear of the cabin, the wing folding backwards on each side from a point just outboard of the fuselage and pivoting to stow vertically, parallel with the fuselage and abutting the tailplane. The

A fictitious all-in-one depicted in both airborne and road-going forms on the cover of the August 1956 issue of *Hobby* magazine.

The same issue features this artwork of the imaginary vehicle taking to the water.

In 1950 Luigi Pellarini filed a patent in the United States regarding the method of folding the wings on his Aernova and Aerauto flying cars.

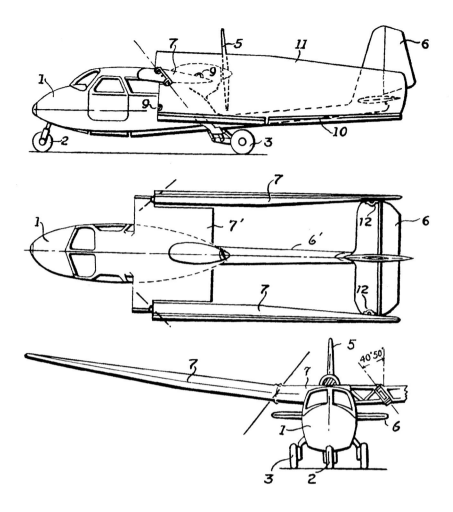

Aeronova was powered by an air-cooled 125bhp Lycoming four-cylinder engine, operating a two-blade 'pusher' propeller at the rear of the wing. The AER 1 was shown at the 1948 Milan Fair and flew for the first time on 9 May 1948, but it never got beyond the prototype stage.

In 1949 a new business was set up, again in Milan, to develop another of Pellarini's projects, the Aerauto PL5C. Powered by a Continental engine of only 85bhp, the Aerauto was a two-seater, and not as fast as the AER 1 – its cruising speed was said to be 100mph, against a claimed 130mph for its predecessor.

The general conception remained the same, but the Aerauto was particularly good-looking. Indeed, the car part was designed by Colli, a respected Milan coachbuilder established in 1932 and best known for its work on Fiat and Alfa Romeo chassis.

The first tests of the Aerauto proved satisfactory. The machine had excellent roadholding, thanks to a movable rear drivetrain: in road-going format the rear wheels slid towards the rear, increasing the wheelbase considerably and bringing the centre of gravity of the powerpack and propeller within the triangle formed by the three wheels. With the wings folded and resting against the tailplane, the machine proved to be aerodynamically very efficient and its on-road performance was excellent. This was all the more so as the rear prop served not only for airborne but also for road-going propulsion; this was one of Pellarini's great innovations.

The machine's behaviour in the air was equally satisfactory, and Luigi Pellarini showed off his Aerauto during a year-long tour of Italy throughout 1950. The crowds gave him a warm welcome and the engineer was soon planning a bigger sister to the Aerauto, the PL6C. This would be a three-seater, equipped with the 125bhp Lycoming engine of the Aernova.

But despite their undeniable media success the Pellarini flying cars were finally seen as dream machines rather than devices to be used in real life, on a daily basis, and on a large scale. In Italy even more than in the United States, in purely commercial terms they failed to attract the investors necessary to take the project forward.

Luigi Pellarini left Europe in the 1950s for Australia and New Zealand, where he developed various new planes, including the Transavia PL-12 Airtruk/Skyfarmer. Intended for crop-spraying, this bizarre machine bore a passing resemblance to the Aerauto, and can be seen on the cinema screen in *Mad Max 3*.

The Fulgar dream car was a fantasy show-car built by French car-maker Simca in 1958. Its equipment supposedly included an electronic 'brain', radar navigation, and rear wings that suggested that the car would be capable of use in the air as well as on the road. It was, said Simca, 'a look into the future that is remarkable for the sobriety of its lines and its European proportions'.

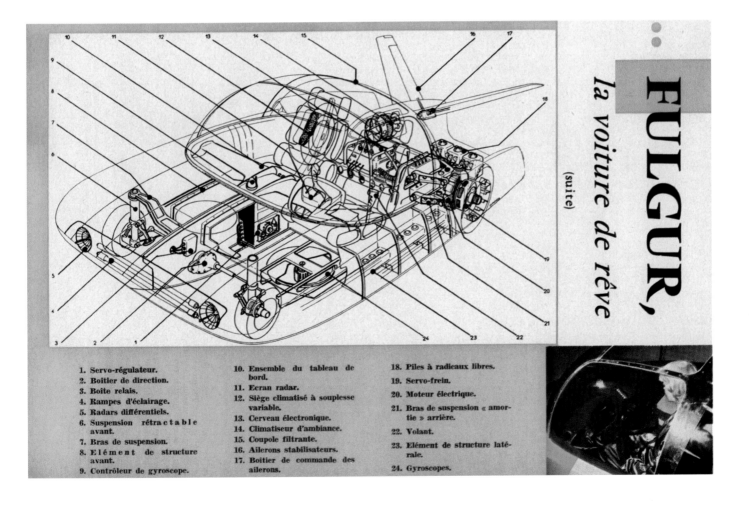

FULGUR, la voiture de rêve (suite)

1. Servo-régulateur.
2. Boîtier de direction.
3. Boîte relais.
4. Rampes d'éclairage.
5. Radars différentiels.
6. Suspension rétractable avant.
7. Bras de suspension.
8. Elément de structure avant.
9. Contrôleur de gyroscope.
10. Ensemble du tableau de bord.
11. Ecran radar.
12. Siège climatisé à souplesse variable.
13. Cerveau électronique.
14. Climatiseur d'ambiance.
15. Coupole filtrante.
16. Ailerons stabilisateurs.
17. Boîtier de commande des ailerons.
18. Piles à radicaux libres.
19. Servo-frein.
20. Moteur électrique.
21. Bras de suspension « amortie » arrière.
22. Volant.
23. Elément de structure latérale.
24. Gyroscopes.

A dream car for the near future: a tongue-in-cheek drawing by Jim Berryman published in 1957 in the *Washington Star*. The machine borrows its wing treatment from the Ford Fairlane and its central headlamp from the Tucker. Flick-out side wings allow it to take to the air. Interested customers were invited to apply to the dealer on Mars!

Pellarini's decision to make the wings fold either side of the tail unit – following the lead of Tampier in France during the 1920s – ended up being adopted in the States, not least by Joseph L. Halsmer, an airline pilot who had a small airfield and workshop in La Fayette, Indiana.

In 1959 Halsmer managed to take to the air in the prototype of what he called his Tandem Engine and Roadable Aircraft – also known as the Aero Car or Aircar. But it was only in 1963 that his Model III demonstrated the true effectiveness of the concept of twin-prop drive – with one propeller at the front and one at the rear – and of having four-wheel running gear akin to a proper car chassis rather than an aircraft-style three-wheel undercarriage.

The dominant theme of American inventors remained that of pivoting wings, as pioneered by Daniel Zuck and Stanley Whitaker on their Plane-Mobile (see Chapter 3). In this mould Henry Clark came up with his 'roadable airplane' in 1949, following in Zuck's wake. Similar was the Versatile 1 of Ohio-based teacher Dr Lewis A. Jackson, which had wings that folded back on to the top of the fuselage. The first single-seater version flew in 1956, and a four-seater was tested in 1964.

The torch of the all-in-one system was carried most brightly by Michigan-based inventor Leland D. Bryan. Over a long period, dating back to 1949 – and via several prototypes and scale models – Bryan perfected a vehicle with wings that folded vertically in two movements, to form a box around the fuselage. The machine was approved for motorway use as a motorcycle, thanks to its three-wheel configuration. It stood out in particular, though, for its dual-purpose propulsion, whereby the

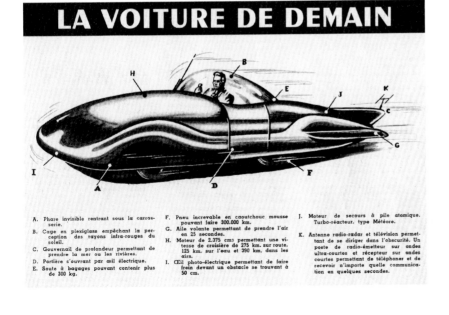

As depicted in the first issue of France's *Science Fiction Magazine*, in 1953, the car of tomorrow would be capable of taking to the air in less than 25 seconds and of flying at 240mph.

propeller was used both in the air and on the road, as with the Aerauto PL5C. Bryan's machine went through three versions before Bryan III met its end at an air-meet at Oshkosh in 1974: one of the wings was not properly secured and folded back on take-off, the resultant crash killing the plane's creator.

As for Bruce K. Hallock of Fenton, Michigan, he was inspired by Waldo Waterman when it came to his Road Wing – but instead went for an all-in-one machine with folding wings. Fourteen years in the building, it flew for the first time in 1957, at Flint, Michigan. The wings and fuselage were in wood, and the four-seater was good for 160mph in the air, courtesy its 145bhp Continental engine. That said, even though the device worked perfectly well in the air and on the road, its state of development still left something to be desired. Once the wings had been folded back, which took about 15 minutes, the size of the propeller prevented road use. The inventor would thus have had to remove the complete wing assembly and take to the road in the fuselage alone, which at the end of the day would have made the Road Wing no different from the Arrowbile of some time before. The Road Wing was thus never used as a car pure-and-simple, and so was closer to an easy-to-park small plane than a flying car. The machine still exists – in store at the Smithville airport in Texas – but hasn't flown for 40 years.

All these models, as we've seen, didn't get beyond the prototype stage. Mostly they were the work of hobbyists rather than bona-fide engineers – let alone people with a business head on their shoulders. As such, they barely left their creator's garage other than to impress the

The Hallock Road Wing (N2721C), built in 1957. The machine was closely inspired by the flying cars of Waldo Waterman. Here Bruce K. Hallock demonstrates how easily the Road Wing can be converted from one form to another.

# Galaxy

## SCIENCE FICTION

**No. 40**

**35¢**

*Price in Great Britain 2/-*

## WANTED—DEAD OR ALIVE by WILLY LEY
## VOLPLA by WYMAN GUIN

**(Crime in Space)**
## A COFFIN FOR JACOB

"But officer, I was only doing Mach 1!" After breaking the speed limit, a flying car is immobilised by a police officer and the driver's documentation inspected. A fantasy scene from a 1956 edition of *Galaxy Science Fiction* magazine.

"Good heavens, honey, have we already arrived at Megapolis?"
Peter confirmed that they had indeed arrived.
"...I just wanted to see what the old banger could manage. 929 kilometres in 13 minutes and..." – he cast a glance at the dashboard – "...and eight seconds," he said. "Not bad for such an old relic!"
He left Janie at their flat. There were a few problems to be sorted before the new lodgers arrived. He landed on the roof of the building where he worked.

Alfred E. van Vogt, Les atomes hantés, *in* SF & Quotidien, *no.3, 1981 (1951).*

odd journalist – and these showed decreasing interest in such devices. The flying car had become a working reality over several years, even if commercial success wasn't around the next corner. But the shock of the new had passed. Furthermore, the attention of the media had turned towards a new 'modular' machine which seemed to have a bright future in front of it: the Aerocar of Molt Taylor.

How to sell youngsters the idea of a flying car (here propelled by a completely hare-brained scientific invention called 'flubber'): the 1961 children's book *The Flying Car*, published by Golden Press and based on the Walt Disney Film *The Absent-minded Professor*.

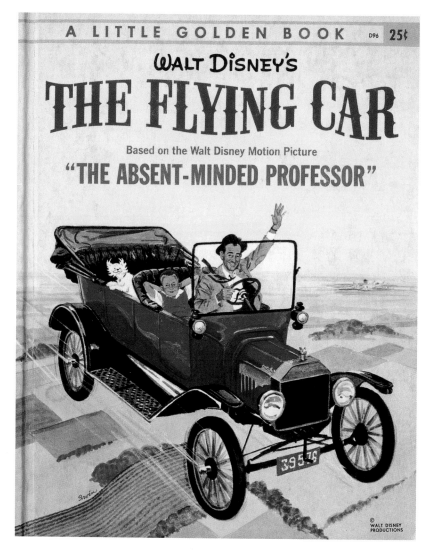

A poster for the film *Chitty Chitty Bang Bang*, which followed *The Absent-minded Professor* as a spectacular production using the idea of a flying car as a way of pulling family audiences into the cinema. The musical inspired by the film is still regularly staged in Britain and the States.

An apparently ordinary car takes to the road...

...before spreading its wings and flying away, in this duo of chromo-lithograph trading cards for a Belgian make of sweets.

**Like a plane without wings**

Rather than developing a car that can be transformed into an aeroplane, why not devise a dual-function machine that always keeps the same form? This was the idea behind the Wingless Plane of William Horton. He built the first prototype, with a single propeller, in 1951, then concentrated on a more powerful twin-prop design, in collaboration with Hughes Aircraft, the company belonging to millionaire Howard Hughes.

Despite its name, the vehicle – at least in its second version – did in fact have wings, albeit just short retractable ones to provide added stability in flight. These folded into the fuselage when the machine was used on the road. Alas, Horton's hopes were soon dashed: after a dispute with Hughes over intellectual property rights, an interminable law case began, in the course of which the Wingless Plane was seized and ultimately destroyed. One of the points of contention concerned the plane's ability to fly, which Hughes contested. Extracts from films discovered since do seem, however, to prove the contrary.

A few years later, inspired by the success of Robert Fulton's Airphibian, Herbert Trautman decided to build his own flying car. Powered by an 85bhp Continental engine, the prototype Road Air was finished in 1959 and bore a strong resemblance to Horton's Wingless Plane. The machine again had short auxiliary wings, placed under the fuselage and deployed when in the air. An original feature was the way the pilot gained access to the cockpit through a hatch at the front of the vehicle. Once the Road Air had been completed, Trautman could hardly wait to test it. He got it up to 90mph on the road and pulled back the joystick. The machine got about three feet off the ground and demonstrated a scary lack of stability. A chastened Trautman swiftly put the device back on the ground and drove it back to its hanger, where it remained untouched, its creator happy to have survived the experience unscathed. The Road Air can be seen today in Florida's 'Fantasy of Flight' museum.

Finally, at the beginning of the 1990s engineer Ken Wernicke revived the idea of a non-transformable flying car, with a similar design (see Chapter 11), but again the venture was unsuccessful.

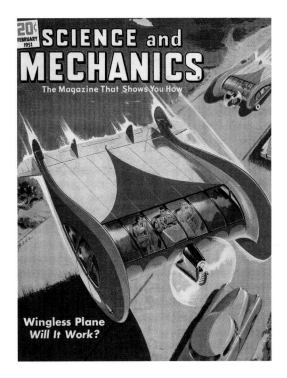

William Horton's Wingless Plane made the cover of *Science and Mechanics* for February 1951. The machine took off from a runway parallel to the motorway, complete with elegantly-dressed passengers.

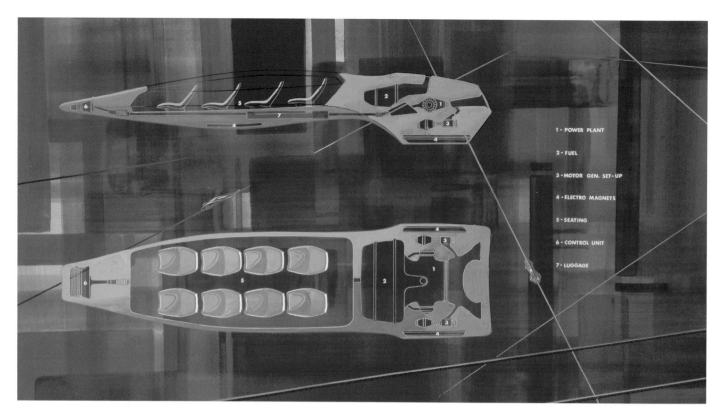

Two pieces of artwork depicting a bus using magnetic levitation, as dreamt up by Frederick J. 'Bud' Magaldi in 1965. These are entirely automated vehicles, capable of carrying eight passengers.

### Resisting gravity

For more than a century the idea of resisting gravity has been a fantasy of science-fiction. H.G. Wells, for example, came up with Cavorite, a material invented by Dr Cavor, as a way of reaching the cosmos in his 1901 novel *The First Men in the Moon*. The idea was taken up again 60 years later in the Walt Disney film *The Absent-Minded Professor*, when a material called flubber ('flying rubber') made it possible for a crack-pot boffin to get his car to fly.

Anti-gravity machines have more to do with imaginary science – magic, even – than with any real-world technology. But never mind that: they represent the same wish to shake of the shackles of reality as do flying cars, even if the latter have at least proved their feasibility.

The illustrations on these two pages are all from the collection of Hampton Wayt. A lover of mid-20th-century automotive design, US-based Wayt has built up an unparalleled collection of artwork and documentation relating to concept cars, including numerous futurist designs that have never seen the light of day.

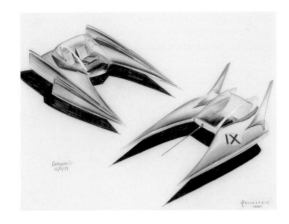

Anti-gravity vehicles drawn in 1957 by Jerry Brochstein, and probably inspired by the hovercraft.

A proposed cover for *Radio Craft* magazine showing vehicles levitating on an electric force-field. In the background can be seen a radio-transmission tower conceived by famed inventor Nikola Tesla and intended for installation on Long Island. The illustration, by Pearsall, dates from approximately 1944.

The passengers of this levitating bus travel under a transparent canopy, one behind the other, in this 1959 drawing by George Anderson.

The second (non commercial) example of the Aerocar, registered N101D, in the air over a suburb near Longview, Washington State, during the mid 1950s.

**8.**

# Molt Taylor and the saga of the Aerocar

The most famous flying car is without a doubt the Aerocar – a modular machine conceived, constructed, put on sale, and improved over 40 years by Moulton 'Molt' Taylor, and which marked an entire generation of Americans at the end of the 1950s.

## The inspiration of the Airphibian

Moulton Taylor was born in 1912. Right from childhood he had a passion for anything that flew. At the minimum legal age of 16 he made his first solo flight. It was no surprise, then, that after brilliant further education – paid for with money earnt as a pianist – that he became an aeronautical engineer.

In 1942 Taylor was mobilised as a reservist in the Navy. As an expert in electronics he worked on several top-secret projects (including the *Gorgon* and *Fox* projects) and helped the development of guidance systems for unmanned planes and missiles. He was the first to make a ground-to-ground missile fly direct to its target, which led to his being promoted to head of the research laboratory which would later introduce the first generation of cruise missiles. At the end of the war he left the Navy as Commander, having been awarded the Legion of Merit decoration.

Whilst on leave during the war, Taylor met Jesse Minnick, a talented mechanic who was as passionate about flying as he was – his first DIY machine had been a sort of winged motorcycle that he had built when still a teenager, and which had proved slightly less than capable when it came to the matter of actually leaving the ground...

Taylor and Minnick got on well together, and in the course of their conversations came to realise that both of them were fascinated by the idea of a machine that could at the same time be driven as a car and flown as an aeroplane. They made up their minds that after the war they would work together to create just such a device. The division of labour was swiftly established: Taylor would look after design and Minnick would build it.

Once demobbed, Taylor started on the development of various planes, in particular the Coot amphibian and then the Imp and Mini-Imp, which were sports single-seaters with an inverted-vee wing. One day Taylor was buying aircraft parts at New Castle in Delaware – with a plan to build a floatplane already christened the Duckling – when he witnessed the smoothly-executed landing of Robert Fulton's Airphibian. He watched with stupor as the pilot unbolted the tail unit and the wing of the machine in no time at all, took to the wheel of what had become, as if by magic, a small motor car, and then drove off the aerodrome.

## Modular and transportable

Taylor was extremely impressed by Fulton's machine – as was the Civil Aeronautics Administration, which would soon afterwards give the Airphibian the necessary clearances to allow it to be put on sale. Taylor gladly recognised that the Airphibian was an undeniable success, but he was convinced he could do better. Because if the principal aim of a flying car was to give its user the freedom to go where and when he wanted, the need to leave the aeroplane parts in a hanger on some aerodrome in order to use the car on the road was a singular brake on that freedom. Taylor's idea was as simple as it was brilliant: the wings, tail unit and propeller would be brought together in the form of a trailer to be towed behind the car.

In February 1948 Molt Taylor founded Aerocar Inc, in Longview, Washington State, with the aim of developing and building a flying car. Taylor thus became an entrepreneur, and began seeking funds. In this he was successful: fifty or so local businessmen allowed themselves to be convinced and each invested a thousand dollars. The money allowed Taylor and Minnick to create a quarter-scale model and test it in the Seattle windtunnel of the University of Washington. The results were satisfying and in July the decision was made to build a full-size prototype. Two engineers were recruited and the first Aerocar emerged from its hanger in the southern suburbs of Longview, during October 1949.

The Aerocar was equipped with a three-speed gearbox and a 100bhp Franklin engine, soon replaced by a 143bhp Lycoming unit. The rear wheels being used for landing, Taylor opted for front-wheel drive for the car. This was an unusual choice. Even if some European constructors, in particular Citroën, had favoured front-drive for a good while, as an avant-garde technical solution that considerably improved comfort and roadholding, in the US it was something hardly ever encountered.

The ground-based tests went well. All that was needed was five minutes – and a simple crank-handle – to unbolt the 34ft wings, the tail section and the propeller, and to transform these elements into a trailer towable by the fuselage, which had now become a small two-seat car. A detail indicative of the creators' wish to devise a vehicle of wide appeal was the accent put on the safety of the user, in particular with a whole range of warning sounds.

*We use the car above all for short journeys. For longer ones we take the plane.*

*You ask whether we envisage building flying cars. Personally, I think that such a car is hardly a rational solution. To make a car into something that flies, you have to make it into a much more complicated machine, and one that will be far more expensive; yet at the same time this would compromise both its road-going and its flying qualities. Such an air-going hybrid would be inferior to a car when on the ground and inferior to a plane when in the sky. Only in certain very specific cases would flying cars have any real use.*

*Serge Gouchrchev, Michel Vassiliev,* La vie au XXIᵉ siècle, *Buchet/Chastel, 1959.*

The Aerocar (here N100D) could reach 110mph in flight.

Mrs Taylor demonstrates the ease of use of the
machine invented by her husband. Here, in front of a
hotel, the Aerocar has its aircraft components in tow.

The prototype Aerocar, N31214 (later registered
N4994P), takes off from near Longview in 1949.

Moulton Taylor poses proudly beside his prototype
Aerocar, sometime during 1949.

## A complicated period of development

Unfortunately the first test flight was short-lived: the propeller fell off.
The risk was a known one. Unlike Fulton, who gave his Airphibian a
front-mounted propeller, directly powered off the engine, Moulton
Taylor was adamant that the prop be fixed on the flying part of the
car, and thus at the rear. On the technical level this considerably complicated things, as the prop had to be linked to the engine via a 10ft
mechanism that traversed the entire tail section. But there were also
advantages – in particular the elimination of airflow problems at the
leading edges of the wings caused by a front-mounted propeller. Equally
to the point, on a practical level this arrangement allowed the owner to
take the two sections apart more easily.

The first official flight of the Aerocar took place on 8 December 1949.
After nine months of further development, it had its first real success,
making a flight from Salem in Oregon to Longview, on 29 August 1950.
In April 1951 it was despatched to Fort Bragg, in North Carolina, to be
assessed by the American army (which ended up preferring the helicopter
as a way of transporting troops) and then it was presented to various
potential private buyers. At the end of these demonstrations, at least 25
people had shown interest in buying an Aerocar. Molt Taylor felt he was
on the road to success; however he still had his work cut out to improve
the design so it could become a valid commercial proposition.

In particular there were numerous attempts to find a solution to
vibration problems in flight. In the end Taylor unearthed a French

patent for a dry-fluid coupling called Flexidyne which used steel shot suspended in gel. Using this put weight up by less than $1/2$ cwt. Thus modified, the prototype proved to have remarkable stability in flight. It could reach a speed of 110mph, with a cruising speed of 100mph and a range of 300 miles. On the road the Aerocar was claimed to be good for 55-60mph, at an average 15mpg, and was quoted as needing 650ft to take off and 300ft to land.

On 15 December 1956 the Aerocar received all the clearances necessary for its sale – making it only the second flying car, after the Airphibian, to be declared legal for highway use as well as in the air. Following on from the prototype, five new Aerocars were laid down, with a retail price fixed at $25,000. But construction remained essentially home-made, Minnick and his small team machining parts by hand.

The Aerocar in its experimental form, parked in the snow in front of Molt Taylor's premises in Longview, during the winter of 1949.

# 3 in one!

**1.** **A COMPLETE AIRCRAFT**

In the air your AEROCAR is a safe, fast, two place, CAA approved* light plane with speed and performance comparable with other aircraft of similar weight and power.

**2.** **FULLY MOBILE**

Land at an airport — and minutes later you are on your way to your **exact** destination with your folded wing-tail trailer in **tow** behind you. Complies with all Motor Vehicle Codes for highway travel.

**3.** **A COMPLETE CAR**

Or leave your wings-tail trailer component behind and your smart little coupe is just the kind of a second automobile you have always wanted for town and business travel.

\* Approved Type Certificate No. 4A16.

## NOW!!
### Available On Order

## From Point

Not only does your AEROCAR get you there faster, but it also does it with greater safety, comfort, and ease. No traffic jams — No weather delays — No road weariness — No Rental-Car problems or Hangar congestion.

AEROCAR is the **only** complete single vehicle that can make the trip from one point to a distant point at higher average speed than a modern automobile.

## to Point!

AEROCAR can **average** better than 90 MPH between points — usually equaling airline time between downtown destinations for distances up to 200 miles. And — you make your own schedules!

Sales catalogue describing the advantages of Molt Taylor's '3 in one' machine – and giving technical details. The catalogue was posted from Longview on 24 March 1958, in the heyday of the Aerocar project.

## SIMPLE OPERATION

Flight and Road operation of an AEROCAR is unsurpassed in simplicity. — Aerodynamic features make flying an AEROCAR like driving. Takeoff and landing on four wheels is safer and far easier than in conventional aircraft — Controls and instruments are arranged in a simple, attractive, familiar automobile dash panel.

## UNSURPASSED UTILITY

AEROCAR is designed for routine daily automobile use — as convenient for the trip down town as for a lengthy flight. AEROCARs have been driven thousands of miles and flown hundreds of hours to develop the ruggedness and simplicity you expect from such a vehicle.

## ATTRACTIVE INTERIOR

Inside — your AEROCAR has all the comfort and attractive appointments of a fine motor car — fashioned by experienced craftsmen using the finest materials — complete in every detail — yet it also has all instruments and safety features found in popular light planes.

## CAR TO PLANE – PLANE TO CAR

The transition from car to plane or plane to car can be accomplished in as little as five minutes by one person. All without the need for special tools or extra equipment, and with little physical effort.

## SMOOTH FLUID DRIVE

A single Model 0-320 143-HP Lycoming Aircraft Engine powers the AEROCAR for both ground and air operation.
Fluid Drive of both the car drive line and the propeller assures smooth, dependable, long life operation with a minimum of service and maintenance problems.

## PERFORMANCE

| | |
|---|---|
| Top Speed | Over 110 MPH |
| Cruise Speed | Over 100 MPH |
| Rate of Climb (@ 2050 Lbs.) | Over 550 FPM |
| Ceiling | 12,000 Ft. |
| Cruise Range (fly) | Over 300 Mi. |
| Landing Speed | 50-55 MPH |
| Landing Run (Braked) | 300 Ft. |
| Take-off Run (Loaded) | 650 Ft. |
| Practical Road Speed (Car) | 55-60 MPH |
| Practical Road Speed (Trailer) | 45-50 MPH |
| Road RPM | 2000 RPM at 50MPH |
| Top Road Speed | 67 MPH at red line |
| Road Range | Over 300 Mi. |
| Fuel Consumption (Fly) | 8 GPH |
| Road Fuel Mileage | 15 MPG |
| Plane to Car Change | 5 Minutes |
| Car to Plane Change | 5 Minutes |
| Rated Flight HP | 143 HP |
| Effective Road HP | 40 HP |
| Stall Speed (@ 2050 Lbs.) | 51 MPH |
| Road Acceleration | 62 MPH - 1/4 Mi. |

Licensed in Normal Category
Acrobatic Maneuvers Prohibited
80-87 Octane Aircraft Fuel Required

## SPECIFICATIONS

| | |
|---|---|
| Car Empty, Weight | 1100 Lbs. |
| Trailer, Weight | 400 Lbs. |
| Design Useful Load | 550 Lbs. |
| Allowed Baggage Weight | 60 Lbs. |
| Wing Span | 34 Ft. |
| Wing Area | 190 Sq. Ft. |
| Wing Loading (@ 2050 Lbs.) | 10.8 Lbs. Sq. Ft. |
| Auto Road Tread | 5' 2" |
| Auto Wheel Base | 6' 8 |
| Trailer Wheel Tread | 5' 2" |
| Car-Trailer Length | 26 Ft. |
| Baggage Space | 14 Cu. Ft. |
| Baggage Space, Width | 36" |
| Tire Size | 4.50 x 12 |
| Trailer Tire Size | 10 x 3.50 x 4 |
| Length (Aircraft) | 21' 6" |
| Height (Car) | 5' 4" |
| Height (Aircraft) | 7' 6" |
| Height (Trailer) | 8' 0" |
| Trailer Length | 15 Ft. |
| Car Length | 10' 4" |
| Seat Width | 44" |
| Power Loading (@ 2050 Lbs.) | 14.3 Lb. HP |
| Car Ground Clearance | 12" |
| Fuel Tank Capacity | 23.5 Gal. |
| Trailer Width | 96" |

## STANDARD EQUIPMENT

Modified, fan cooled Lycoming 0-320 Horizontal Opposed, 4 cylinder aircraft engine. Derated to 143 H.P.

All engine and flight instruments required for CAA certification.

Speedometer with Odometer.

Engine Hourmeter.

Nickle Cadmium Lifetime Battery. (12-volt) With push button starting.

Special Heavy Duty Generator with voltage regulator.

Geared Starter with Torque limited Folo-thru drive.

Dual Magnetos with automatic spark advance, shielded, with locking ignition switch.

Roll Down Windows with wind wings on locking doors, both sides.

Cigarette Lighter and Ash Tray.

Safety Instrument Panel with extra instrument and radio provision.

Locking Gas Cap on Cell Type Fibreglas Fuel Tank.

Two tinted windshield visors.

All lights required for night flight and Motor Vehicle Code requirements.

Speed controlled blower for fresh and/or hot cabin air.

Dual electric windshield wipers.

Electric Horn.

Thermostatic Oil Radiator Control.

Two-tone Enamel Auto Paint on Fibreglas Car Body.

Built-in Radio Antennas.

Carburetor Air Cleaner.

Two-tone Vinyl Interior Upholstery and Headlining. Sponge Rubber Seat Cushions with no-sag springs.

Pilot and Passenger Shoulder Harness and Safety Belts.

Tufted Rubber backed Floor Rug.

Safety Rear View Mirror.

Safety Steering Wheel.

Fingertip Flashing Turn Signal Control.

Standard Automotive Three Speed Gear Box with Reverse.

Built-in Retractable Wheels and Jacks on Trailer.

Fluid Drive Auto Driveline and Propeller Shaft.

Rubber Mounted Drivelines, with Lifetime Sealed Bearings.

Stainless Steel Decorative Trim.

Ball Joint Front Wheel Suspension with Front Wheel Drive.

Stainless Steel Control Cables, Ball and Needle Bearing Controls.

Weather Protected Car Frame.

Expander Tube Hydraulic Brakes.

Automatic Flight Control and Propeller Shaft Hook-up.

Folding Wings of all metal construction.

Stainless Tipped, Plastic, Ground Adjustable Propeller with Spinner Cap.

Hard Plexiglas Wrap-around Windshield with Safety "pop-out" mounting.

Wheel Mounted Fenders.

Gravity Fuel Flow with Metal Gascolator Bowl and Filter.

Stall Warning Indicator, operates car horn.

Coil Spring with Hydraulic Shock Absorber Auto Suspension.

Safety Interlock Switches to starter on all Wings — Tail attach points.

Dual Flight Controls.

Combination Foot and Hand Throttle Linkage.

Parking Brake with Warning Light.

Additional Equipment, Including Radio and Special Instruments available on order.

Separate Clutch, Brake and Rudder Pedals.

Safety Automatic Flight Control Unlock.

Note how the wings-tail component of the AEROCAR folds into a compact trailer for road travel. The built-in trailer wheels retract into the wing leading edge during flight.

The AEROCAR has been designed for daily automotive use and has been under constant development and test for over eight years. This experience permits us to now offer a highly perfected vehicle with hundreds of hours of flight—and thousands of miles of driving background.

You can expect your AEROCAR to give service and utility without special expensive maintenance. AEROCARS are guaranteed for the first 25,000 miles of travel on a parts replacement basis.

Present facilities permit only limited production of AEROCARS. You can now own a custom-built AEROCAR and enjoy the many advantages of AEROCAR travel. At the same time you can have the benefit of the terrific attraction value of early AEROCAR ownership for your own advertising and promotion activity.

We are now accepting orders. Price and delivery quotations will be furnished on request.

First in Autonautics!

AEROCARS are built in our own plant under U. S. Patent No. 2,767,939 with other patents pending.

Manufactured by

### AEROCAR
INC.

LONGVIEW, WASHINGTON

# AEROCAR
## The Car With The Built-in Freeway!

Watched in wonderment by a robot, a flying car threads between a line of fuel stacks in the future-world depicted on the cover of this German science-fiction title in the *Terra* series (volume 542, Moewig, 1967).

In *Aventures Fiction*, a collection of 'comic strips for adults', the passengers of a flying car are confronted by strange extra-terrestial creatures (Arédit, October 1969).

### An American star

With the machine's homologation in his top pocket, Moulton Taylor now had to work on promoting the Aerocar, and so he began a vast tour of the country. The Aerocar participated in a number of air shows and car rallies, and appeared regularly on television. The most memorable appearance was without a doubt on *I've got a Secret*: Taylor arrived on stage at the wheel of a small car which three minutes later reappeared transformed into a plane, in front of a public which couldn't believe its eyes. At the end of the 1950s the Aerocar was at the peak of its fame.

The comedian Bob Cummings was the first person to buy an Aerocar, in 1960, and Moulton Taylor personally took charge of its delivery, this being the first commercially-produced example, registered N102D. On the way, he stopped at an Earl Scheib drugstore. After checking that the paint he was about to purchase was 'guaranteed for all car-body use' he bought big pots of both yellow and green, and repainted the Aerocar in the livery of Nutra-Bio, the vitamin-maker that sponsored the famous *Bob Cummings Show*. Thus transformed into a first-rate publicity vehicle, the Aerocar appeared regularly on the programme.

Registered N103D, the second production Aerocar was sold to a Mr Whitebrecht of Massachusetts. He was a great fan of air shows and never missed an occasion to demonstrate the performance of the Aerocar. In this manner he ended up in Havana a little after Castro came to power. Fidel's brother Raúl went for a short test flight over Cuba with Whitebrecht, but the Aerocar had a petrol problem and had to put down on a stretch of country road. One of the wings was damaged, and an improvised repair had to be made by cutting strips of metal from a jerrycan. Thus held-together, N103D made it back to Boston. Whitebrecht sold the Aerocar to a Chrysler dealer in Philadelphia who for a time put it on show as a curiosity.

The problem was that the Aerocar was too expensive for the general public. Molt Taylor recognised this: for what the machine cost, buyers expected a real car (a four-seater, in other words) and didn't really want to make any effort when it came to converting the machine, even if it was generally only a matter of a quarter of an hour – if everything went well, because the operation could easily take 45 minutes on rough ground or if aligning the two sections proved difficult. But Taylor's aim wasn't to retail the Aerocar himself; rather he hoped to sell the licence to a manufacturer of cars or planes.

Convinced that this way the Aerocar would take off commercially, Molt Taylor began negotiations with Dallas-based industrial group Ling-Temco-Vought with a view to beginning mass-production. The two parties reached a deal. The Texans agreed to build a thousand Aerocars and on that basis to supply them to Taylor at a price of $8500 a piece – leaving him to sell them on at between $10,000 and $12,000. But there

was one non-negotiable condition: Taylor had to provide firm orders for 500 machines and lay down a $500,000 deposit.

Impossible? Not for Taylor, who started setting up a network of concessionaires by prospecting aircraft sellers around the country. These were tasked with finding customers and offering them the Aerocar at a retail price of $14,000. Taylor was convinced that things would soon be buttoned up.

In the interim the famed N103D – the Aerocar that had flown over Cuba – had been sold back to Aerocar International by its new owner. After being brought up to as-new condition, the company sold it swiftly to KISN, a Portland, Oregon, radio station. The machine was entrusted to journalist Allyn Merris so he could report on traffic conditions direct from the skies. Between his slots on the radio, Merris amused himself with the difficult art of frightening seagulls with the notably strident horn and impressing passengers with demonstrations of the turn indicators...

Painted in lurid colours, Molt Taylor's flying car became an object of popular culture when star of the small screen Bob Cummings decided to use it for his TV show in 1961. You could even buy a model kit to make a miniature Aerocar in the comfort of your own home!

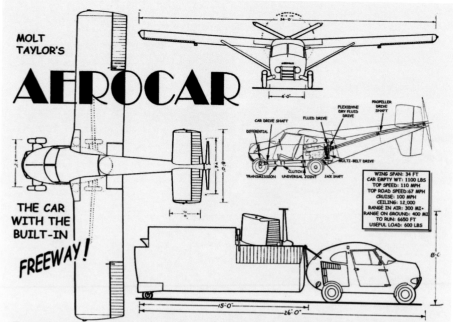

The concept of vehicles that could transform themselves from automobiles to airplanes dates back to the earliest days that the two both existed. The ubiquitous Glenn Curtiss produced a design for a three-seat flying car in time for the Pan-American Aeronautic Exposition in New York in February 1917. It flew, but poorly, and was scrapped. Subsequent literature ranges from stories of back-yard tinkerers to the fantasies that Ian Fleming imagined to get James Bond out of tight situations.

Taylor was a gifted aeronautical engineer, "crazy about airplanes" from adolescence. In 1942, as a Naval reservist, he became the first person to successfully "fly" a surface-to-surface missile to its target, and the following year, as a lieutenant commander, he headed the project that produced the first generation of cruise missiles.

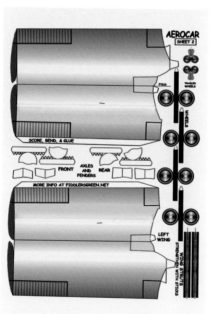

A paper model of the Aerocar (available on www.fiddlersgreen.net): even today the machine remains a source of fascination to many Americans.

**Down to earth with a bump…**

Just when everything seemed to be going for the best, the wind turned. In 1962 CBS did not renew Robert Cummings's contract. With his programme off the air, he sold N102D back to Molt Taylor's company. At the same time KISN replaced its Aerocar, which had all the same racked up over 1000 hours of reporting time, with a normal light aircraft. In use, the machine had been shown to lack power: in particularly hot weather it had been difficult to gain altitude, and on several occasions the Aerocar had flatly refused to leave the ground.

N103D was bought, via a dealer in secondhand planes, by an enthusiastic amateur pilot in Mosyrock, Washington, who for a time used it for his professional travels, on behalf of Procter & Gamble. After an accident it was repaired by Taylor, keeping the plane part but replacing the front end with that of N100D, which he had retained as a demonstrator, and fitting the engine from N103D. Sold on several times, Aerocar N103D is no longer air-worthy – it flew for the last time in 1977 – but is kept in the private collection of the Felling family, in Colorado. For several years it has been on the market, but has not yet found a buyer, despite the asking price having been reduced to $2.2m.

As for the planned mass-production of the Aerocar by Ling-Temco-Vought, that hung fire. Taylor managed to pull in 278 firm orders, each accompanied by a deposit. He thus had more than $250,000 dollars in capital, but that wasn't deemed sufficient by LTV, which refused to lower its requirements. Thus, thanks to a shortfall of 222 orders production never began and the deal was never consummated. Moulton Taylor had no alternative but to wait for better times to revive his dream of a flying car.

Of the five hand-made 'production' models laid down after the initial prototype, four were finally completed. Hence five Aerocars in total saw the light of day, between 1948 and 1962, all with a Lycoming engine but with varying power outputs, these often being uprated on an evolutionary basis. Today the prototype is in Oshkosh, Wisconsin, the property of the Experimental Aircraft Association, while the others are in private hands.

**The Aerocar III**

During the 1960s Molt Taylor built other aircraft, and in 1967 one of them was called Aerocar II. But this was an orthodox plane, a light four-seater. However, at the same time he continued to work on a new modular machine, and the sole prototype, called the Aerocar III, took to the air for the first time in June 1968.

Whilst Aerocar I had hardly been an aesthetic success, the automotive element of Aerocar III, in glassfibre and finished in red, was altogether

*I bought a brand-new air-mobile*
*It was custom-made, it was a Flight De Ville*
*With a powerful motor and some hideaway wings*
*Push in on the button and you will get a scene.*

*Now you can't catch me*
*No, baby you can't catch me*
*'Cause if you get too close,*
*You know I'm gone like a cool breeze…*

*I put my foot in my tank and I began to roll*
*Moanin' siren, it was a state patrol*
*So I let out my wings and then I blew my horn*
*Bye bye New Jersey, I'd become airborne.*

*Now you can't catch me*
*No, baby you can't catch me*
*'Cause if you get too close,*
*You know I'm gone like a cool breeze…*

*"You Can't Catch Me", Chuck Berry, 1956.*

The Aerocar III, with its more elegant design, attracted the attention of the Ford Motor Company in 1970. But Ford's interest was transitory and no further version of the MkIII was to see the light of day. The sole example built is today the property of the Museum of Flight in Seattle.

sleeker. There were numerous technical improvements, even although Aerocar III incorporated elements of the earlier model – for which reason it carried the N100D serial number of the first 'production' Aerocar. The wheels, bigger than those on Aerocar I, were henceforth retractable in flight, which improved aerodynamics. The engine developed 143bhp, and on the road it powered the front wheels through fluid-coupling reduction gearing that brought power down to 40bhp. The braking system was derived from that conceived by B.F. Goodrich for the B-52 bomber, and allowed the Aerocar to land in a distance of less than 100 yards. The aircraft section was all-aluminium, and weight-saving and an increase in power gave a clear performance advantage to this version of the Aerocar.

Unfortunately, owing to changes in legislation the machine now needed no fewer than eight certificates of conformity before it could be put on the market. That wasn't enough to deter the Ford Motor Company from taking a close interest. Success seemed at last to be in reach for Taylor.

The dynamic Lee Iacocca, at the time president of Ford's North American operations, instructed Donald Petersen, vice-president of the research division – and future CEO – and Richard Place, another company high-up, and in addition the holder of a pilot's licence, to meet Moulton Taylor at his Longview home. In August 1970 Richard Place made a test flight at the controls of the Aerocar III. He was sufficiently impressed by the machine's performance to advise his hierarchy to carry out some more detailed market research.

But Ford's enthusiasm waned. The official reason for this sudden loss of interest was the strong growth in the importation of Japanese cars, providing strong competition for bottom-of-range American models, and the beginning of the Fuel Crisis with its consequences of raised production costs and the falling away of demand for bigger 'gas-guzzlers'. Informally, it was also said that the ambitious Donald Petersen didn't want to put his career in danger by supporting a project that was a bit too out of the ordinary and could even have been judged loony.

The coup de grace came when the Ford men in company with Molt Taylor visited the Federal Aviation Administration to talk about their possible mass-production of a flying car. When they mentioned the possibility of making several thousand examples each year (an internal report spoke of potential sales of 15,000 per year) the FAA delegate was hardly bowled over with enthusiasm. He replied that obtaining the necessary certification for producing something for such a large market would not be plain sailing, and hinted that the process would be long and extremely expensive. A favourable outcome would be by no means a foregone conclusion.

The risk seemed too great for Ford, because the company had been seeking significant Federal support, and even a government stake in the project. Once again, the hoped-for partner to make and sell the Aerocar on a large scale had chosen not to go through with the venture.

The Aerocar III, after numerous appearances at air shows up until the beginning of the 1980s, can now be found, as with so many of these hybrids, in a museum: in this case, Seattle's Museum of Flight.

Moulton Taylor, meanwhile, headstrong and indefatigable, went back to his drawing-board to design a new generation of flying cars. For Aerocar IV his approach changed. Henceforth the idea was to equip a regular production car – a Honda CRX coupé or a Geo Metro (Suzuki Swift in Europe) – with an ultra-lightweight flying element. A gas-turbine would be fitted inside the tail section and would action a rear-mounted propeller. The aircraft part of the vehicle would be sold by Taylor in kit form, the purchaser thus becoming the constructor of the vehicle – which, from the legal point of view put the machine in the category of experimental planes built by private individuals as a hobby. But success was not around the corner.

After a half-century of nose-to-the-grindstone work, and in spite of some undeniable technical breakthroughs, Moulton Taylor hadn't made a dime with his machines, even if as a result of the publicity it garnered the Aerocar had come to symbolise the flying car, at least for the great American public.

Still, at least the hefty profit Taylor made on selling the Longview premises, bought at the end of the 1940s as a site for his hangar, assured him a comfortable retirement during the course of which he declared himself happy to have never been injured despite spending so many years risking his neck to test his prototypes.

All the evidence is that Moulton Taylor, who died in 1995, is the man who went the furthest in making a reality of the dream of a flying car.

'Your flying car is here today' proclaimed the cover of the December 1951 issue of *Motor Trend* magazine, referring to an article on the Aerocar.

Aerocar III in front of the hangar at Longview. The machine flew for the first time in 1968, and achieved an average speed of 120mph. On the ground it was capable of a rather more modest 50mph.

*But how, you ask, could a car have managed to fail me? (...)*
*I was twenty minutes out of Triangle Lake on my way to the Wiggly River loging region, flying at an altitude of a thousand feet. (...)*
*Then a roc swooped down on me, wrapped ten huge talons around my car, and swallowed it.*

Larry Niven, Safe at any speed,
in Fantasy and Science Fiction, May 1967.

Hardly astonishing, really, to see a flying car make an appearance in a James Bond film, in this case a modified American Motors Matador in 1974's *The Man with the Golden Gun*.

**9.**

# The wilderness years

After the commercial failure of the well-conceived projects of Robert Fulton and Molt Taylor, disenchantment set in. The optimism of the Baby Boom years gave way to a period marked by unfortunate accidents and an ever more restrictive legal environment. The vision of a plane in every garage seemed more distant than ever.

**The sad seventies**

If the inventors of flying cars were often regarded as inveterate dreamers, the pursuit of their dreams was not without danger, and during the 1970s two fatal accidents hit hard at this informal group, costing the lives of Henry Smolinski, and his partner Hal Blake (see p139) and Leland Bryan. Added to the death of pioneer Waldo Waterman and the destruction by fire of the San Diego Aerospace Museum, with the loss of Ted Hall's Roadable Airplane, this period marked a clear watershed in the history of flying cars.

Even on the purely theoretical level, very few projects were the objects of patent applications during that same decade. At the beginning of the 1980s it was thus a legitimate question to ask whether the very concept of a flying car was something of the past. But while the US seemed to be treading water, France kept the torch burning, for a time, with the machine created by Robert Lebouder.

**The Autoplane of Robert Lebouder**

In 1968, while on his way to his summer holidays, Parisian engineer Robert Lebouder thought it would be more agreeable to get to his chosen seaside resort a little bit more quickly. He considered buying a plane, but realised that then he'd have to find a means of getting around once he'd landed.

From that point, over several years and with no aeronautical knowledge, he built the one-off Autoplane, a 'modular' in the spirit of Robert Fulton's Airphibian – doing all the work in his back garden. The machine was based around a little rear-engined Vespa 400 runabout which was clothed in a home-built fuselage.

In summer 1976 Lebouder took his family to Biarritz in the machine, which he had managed to get homologated and which proved to have more than satisfactory performance: over 40mph on the road and up to 110mph in flight. Equipped with two engines, the original Vespa 400 two-stroke moved to the front and a 100bhp Continental at the rear, the Autoplane, which had separate controls for road and air use, racked up 170 hours of flying time over four years, before an over-ambitious take-off broke the undercarriage.

Robert Lebouder gave up using his machine at this point and sold it to one of his friends, Philippe Frange. Today no longer in a flying state, the Autoplane was displayed at the 2005 edition of the Rétromobile classic-car show in Paris.

Starting in 1968, Frenchman Robert Lebouder undertook the construction of a flying car in the garden of his suburban house.

His Autoplane, based on a Vespa 400 runabout, was homologated in 1976, and was used principally to go on holiday.

The Autoplane was a modular machine close in concept to Robert Fulton's Airphibian. The entire flying section could be left in the hanger, the pilot/driver then taking to the road in the cabin-*cum*-car.

By the beginning of the 1960s the flying car was already old-hat in science-fiction – good for the scrapyard, even, judging by this illustration by Ed Emsh for a 1960 edition of *Galaxy Magazine*.

Twenty-five years after the film *The Fifth Element*, the police, in its flying cars, pursue a criminal above a futuristic townscape in a 1971 title (no.174) in the German *Terra Nova* science-fiction series published by Moewig.

In this comic strip in *Magnus* (no.14) a flying car is highly useful to make an escape (Editions des Remparts, 1972).

## A burdensome legal environment

During the 1970s the United States became more and more litigation-happy. People sued over the most trifling things and often won considerable damages for grossly exaggerated and even totally imaginary ills. The only real winners were the lawyers and legal-eagles. The democratic principle of consumer rights was being turned on its head. This lawyers-with-everything society eventually led to the notion of risk being deemed purely and simply unacceptable. With the slightest incident leaving one exposed to substantial damages, experimentation became a far too costly luxury to be given house room. Yet every innovation carries with it an element of the unknown – and sometimes that could be anything but negligible. The tyranny of zero-risk behaviour leads without fail to stagnation...

In this climate the aero industry had to put draconian measures in place to avoid law suits and to conform to ever-more-restrictive legislation. This prevented the expression of any inventiveness and caused the collapse of certain businesses. For safety reasons, Cessna had to stop manufacture of planes powered by a single-cylinder engine, while Piper suffered serious financial problems. Thousands of jobs across the country were lost as a direct consequence of government decisions and the development of a risk-averse society.

In this context, it became almost impossible in the US of the time to obtain the certifications and authorisations necessary to sell new types of light plane to the general public.

## A paradoxical situation

This industrial and commercial stagnation nevertheless had an unexpected consequence: almost all new ideas and technological advances in aeronautics in these last 30 years have been in the domain of experimental aviation.

This was subject to a very particular set of laws, far less restrictive and less open to judicial pursuit. In effect federal American law said that if at least 51% of the work of construction – even if this was merely final assembly followed by adjustments – were carried out by the buyer, he would be legally considered the builder of his own machine. This made it difficult to seek restitution through the courts for any problem linked for example to poor-quality design. The buyer of the kit could not easily launch proceedings against the maker: having put the device together himself made him alone its constructor, in the eye of the law.

A number of innovative flying machines – often using sophisticated technologies – were thus launched in kit form. As a consequence, while the market for small series-production aircraft shrank, the building of experimental prototypes gathered speed.

### The Ten Commandments for building the ideal flying car

1. Thou shalt carry in permanence thy equipment
2. Thou shalt be able to reach a speed of 70mph on the road
3. Thou shalt use only a traditional form of propulsion
4. Thou shalt use only petrol as a fuel
5. Thou shalt be able to park in a standard parking space
6. Thou shalt take off and land horizontally
7. Thou shalt be able to deploy your wings and take off when on the road
8. Thou shalt be able to carry a load of 7.5cwt
9. Thou shalt have a range of 600 miles in the air
10. Thou shalt attain a speed of 180mph in flight

*Comments*

1. *The flying gear needs to be immediately to hand, so you can take off from the nearest airstrip without having to go and fetch anything from a garage or aerodrome hangar.*
2. *To be able to use motorways and freeways.*
3. *To avoid decapitating pedestrians with your propeller whilst on the road.*
4. *For reasons of cost and availability.*
5. *To be able to use a normal garage and public parking spaces.*
6. *Whilst vertical take-off is more practical and more impressive, it is however more complex and uses a lot of power.*
7. *So as to be able to escape your pursuers without having to stop to convert your vehicle – meaning deploying the wings at perhaps 40mph and taking off at 70mph. Technically, taking off from a motorway would therefore be possible, although the legal implications would need to be examined...*
8. *The idea here is to be able to carry four people, including the driver – or to take off on holiday with your girl-friend or boy-friend and sufficient luggage...*
9. *The United States is a big country!*
10. *If not, what's the point in having a plane?*

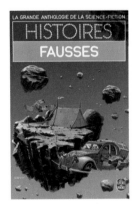

Even a Citroën 2CV can be a star of science-fiction, as on this cover by Adamov for *Histoires Fausses*, a title in the Livre de Poche series *La grande anthologie de la science-fiction* (1984).

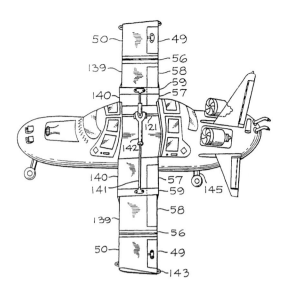

The 1986 patent in the name of Joseph N. Ayoola, for his 'Air, Sea and Land Vehicle'.

This commercial evolution was accompanied by a similar increase in the number of patents taken out for new flying cars or 'roadable aircraft'. More than a dozen applications were filed during the 1980s, and this trend was to accelerate in the following decade.

**Touring the patent jungle...**

'Folding and telescopic' – that was the battle cry of the time, if you sift through the patents taken out. Thus Harvey R. Miller proposed stowing the wings, tail unit and propeller installation in the sides and

Gerry Anderson, father of such famous TV puppet series as *Thunderbirds*, came up with a number of flying cars, not least the Supercar of the series of the same name, in 1961, and the car of Joe McClaine in 1968's *Joe 90*. The latter, here as a Dinky Toys model, had automatically-opening wings.

in the rear compartment of his 'Combined Road Vehicle and Aircraft' of 1981. Allegedly even easier to convert was the 1984 'Pusher Type Autoplane' with its folding wings, proposed by a certain Harry Einstein – who did not state in his patent deposition whether he was related to Albert Einstein or not. Then there was the 1986 patent for an 'Air, Sea and Land Vehicle' lodged by Joseph N. Ayoola. This was a flying amphibious car equipped with two jet engines and with telescopic wings that additionally had sections that folded up accordion-fashion. Even more radical was another Harvey R. Miller creation, 1991's 'Combined Road and Aircraft Vehicle', whose wings folded back lengthways along the chassis to become the body sides of the car, while the telescopic tail section slid forward to enclose the propeller at the rear of the cabin. As for the 'Combined Aircraft and Road Vehicle' of Joseph J. Szakacs (1992), its ultra-flat and heavily glazed rectangular form, three wheels and twin rear airscrews made it a machine worthy of a Gerry Anderson TV series.

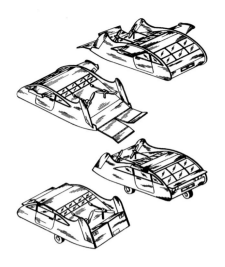

The 'Combined Aircraft and Road Vehicle' of Joseph J. Szakacs, for which a patent application was lodged in 1992.

In spite of this avalanche of vehicles that were to a greater or lesser degree folding, the concept of modularity, which was the general trend 30 years earlier, was by no means dead and buried.

Thus even if Roger Williamson's 1982 'Land Vehicle and Aircraft Combination' looked just like an ordinary twin-engined aircraft, it literally hatched a small car with its own engine and normal road equipment. To do this, all you had to do was lift up the tail of the machine. The cabin was then detached from the floor, which was in reality a simple forward platform. The wheels appeared and the 'car' part could happily hit the road, while the aircraft 'shell' was put away in its hangar.

Karl Eickmann, an American living in Japan, meanwhile came up with the astonishing 'Airborne Vehicle with Hydraulic Drive and Control' of 1989. This had one pair of propellers at the front and another pair at the rear, mounted on tilting wings, and was intended to be able to take off from any highway. And if these four propellers were to prove insufficient, you could always increase to eight the number of airscrews.

Even more surprising was the 1989 'Land, Water and Air Craft' of Harold L. Thompson, a single-seater that looked as if it had come straight from one of Albert Robida's sketchpads. A high-tech look and an obsession with economy were key features, the patent specifying the use of a motorcycle engine, 'this being economical in use of fuel and easy to maintain'. Even more sparse was Peter J. Fitzpatrick's 1990 'Vehicle for Use on Land, Air or Water': you almost felt tempted to look for a set of pedals and a bicycle chain to drive the propeller on this ultra-light off-road vehicle, which was entirely folding. Whether or not it could fit in the boot of a large car wasn't said...

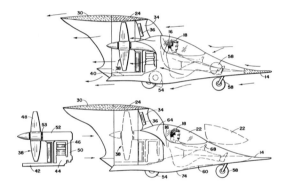

A 1989 patent drawing for the 'Land, Water and Air Craft' of Harold L. Thompson.

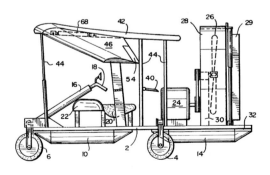

Dating from 1990, this patent drawing is of Peter J. Fitzpatrick's 'Vehicle for Use on Land, Air or Water'.

The flying DeLorean, a creation of mad scientist Doc Brown, allowed Michael J. Fox to travel in time in the Robert Zemeckis film *Back to the Future* (1985).

*'There's no air in space. Cars are a bit leaky, aren't they?'*
*'It only look like a normal car. Thus it will run normally on your roads, using a miniaturised engine powered by reaction mass. The design was highly inefficient before. But the exhaust pipes are really blocked, and the whole body is airtight–for flight. It is even proofed again radiation. The air conditioner stores enough air for four humans for six hours. This replenishes itself whenever the airtight doors are opened –'*
*Alien elephant-tortoise as used car salesman... (...) the creature jerked the steering wheel back with an audible snap. The wheel tilted freely like a joystick. (...) The Thunderbird quivered and hummed; then jumped in the air, tilting at the clear sky.*

Ian Watson, Miracle Visitors, *Reader Union,*
*'SF Book Club', 1979.*

This whistle-stop tour of the patents of the time gives a rough idea of the trends in flying-vehicle design. However the majority of these projects were more sci-fi dreaming than anything technically feasible. With the exception of the odd device knocked up in a domestic garage by a lone inventor – Lebouder's Autoplane, for instance – this was not a fruitful time: not a single flying car patented between 1964 and 1987 took to the air.

In such a context it was hardly a surprise that science-fiction – so often the motor of our dreams – took the driving seat at the beginning of the

The first scene of the film *Heavy Metal* by Gerald Potterton (1981) has a Chevrolet Corvette crossing space to the tune of hot guitar licks...

1980s: the flying car returned in force to screens and comic strips, as a recurring motif of the near-future, as if sci-fi writers were desperately trying to reignite a desire for such vehicles.

As well as presenting a car crossing the cosmos to the tune of guitar riffs in the film *Heavy Metal*, science-fiction warmed the cockles of lovers of hybrid vehicles with two extraordinary devices: the famous time-travelling DeLorean in *Back to the Future*, and above all the flying machines in *Blade Runner*. The film depicted a Los Angeles sky in 2019 given over to 'Spinners', superb vertical-take-off creations conceived by artist Syd Mead, a lover of futurist automobile projects.

But it was unfortunately far more complicated to make a car fly when you took away the special effects.

Ridley Scott's 1982 film *Blade Runner* immortalised so-called 'spinners' – vertical-take-off cars dreamt up by Syd Mead.

Syd Mead's Baroque Beta Mach 7, an anti-gravity limousine created in 1959 for Ford, to decorate the US offices of the company – whose name can be seen in stylised form at the top left of the image. Floating on an electric charge, the machine is depicted surrounded by dignitaries, doubtless on another planet or in a far-distant future.

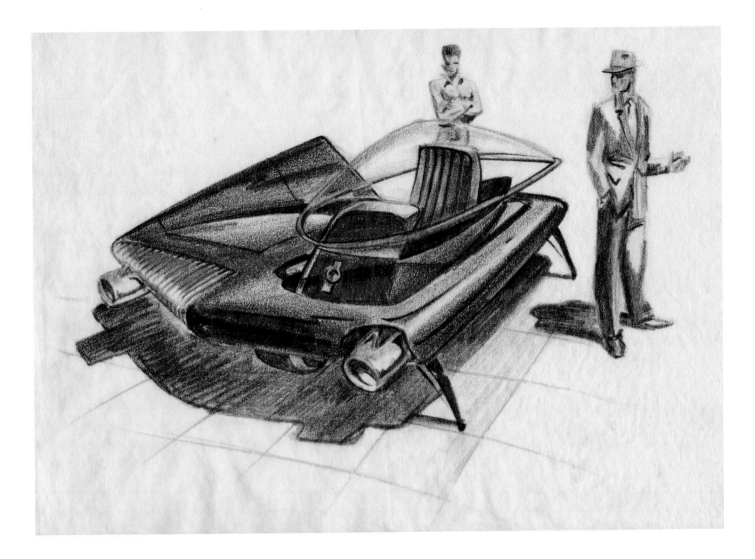

In 1957 illustrator Sydney J. Mead, then still a student at the Art Center College of Design in Pasadena, drew his first private flying cars, these still retaining the basic look of a motor car.

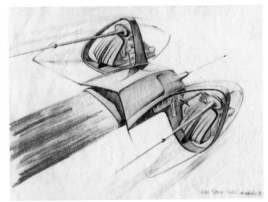

### A hybrid of Beetle and duck

Let's return to practical considerations. In terms of aerodynamics as well as of the principles of physics behind a motor car and an aircraft, it has to be said that these two machines have little in common. A small plane is made up of a cabin with a propeller at the front, a single wing, and a long fuselage with a tail unit, the whole resting on a three-point undercarriage; a small car, on the other hand, comprises a passenger compartment generally with a wheel at each corner and an engine – in most cases – at the front. The only points in common are the existence of a cabin and a front-mounted power unit. That's not much to bring to the party, if you're trying to achieve a happy marriage and a fine hybrid offspring.

Does that mean that the very concept of a flying car is a nonsense? Not necessarily. With cars as with planes there are different ways of doing things – real alternatives to the received orthodoxy. Consider the Volkswagen Beetle. With its rear engine, the Beetle was diametrically opposed to dominant technical practices. But that didn't stop it from becoming the most popular vehicle of all time, ahead even of the legendary Ford Model T.

In the same way an alternative model exists in the aircraft world: the 'Canard'. The main wing is at the rear of the fuselage – and the latter is very short, being between a third and a half the length of the wing. The engine is also at the back, as is the propeller. Finally a small additional wing (called the 'canard wing' – hence the machine's name) is positioned

The craziest car in the world was a flying VW Beetle, according to the Rudolf Zehetgruber film *Das verrückteste Auto der Welt* (1975).

Car manufacturers often used science-fiction as a way of promoting their products: here Volkswagen and its Beetle are the stars of *Mit dem VW zur Venus* (Caprice, 1961).

at the very front of the fuselage – which means that the plane has four lifting surfaces, one at each 'corner'. Although the Wright Brothers plane was a 'Canard', this layout was almost immediately abandoned in favour of the configuration which we know today. Almost no aircraft of 'Canard' type, civil or military, has made it to production.

During the 1980s it was possible all the same to observe a genuine resurgence in interest for this interesting design alternative. The man mainly responsible for the 'Canard' revival was Elbert L. Rutan. A real visionary, Burt Rutan dreamt up some truly revolutionary machines. Later he came up with the Voyager, the ultra-light machine that in December 1986 achieved the first round-the-world flight without landfalls or fuel stops, and SpaceShipOne, the first private spaceship in history.

Before this, Burt Rutan developed several 'Canard' planes, including the Vari-Eze and the Long-EZ, and began by selling plans before offering these as DIY kits. He attracted a number of imitators, including Danny Maher, the inventor of the Velocity, today one of the most popular 'Canards' among home-build enthusiasts.

To be sure, a 'Canard' isn't a flying car – no more than the Beetle, other than in certain films. But perhaps the solution to the fundamental conceptual problem behind the flying car can be found in an amalgam of the 'Canard' type of plane with a car of Beetle-like design. Certainly the fuselage of a 'Canard' is roughly the same length as a small car, the two machines both have a rear-mounted engine, and finally the four lifting surfaces are equivalent to the four wheels of a car. Other than in detail, the evidence points to a strong geometric convergence. The two machines are born of the same aesthetic.

In October 1984 SpaceShipOne, the first private spaceship in history, created by Burt Rutan, took with it into space a handwritten note by Jules Verne.

**A homage to the imaginary as a source of inspiration**

On 4 October 2004 at Switzerland's Maison d'Ailleurs, a museum in Yverdon-les-Bains devoted to science-fiction, utopia and extraordinary voyages, collector Jean-Michel Margot and adventurer Steve Fossett sent a handwritten note by Jules Verne into space, aboard SpaceShipOne.

After its first successful flight on 29 September 2004, SpaceShipOne repeated its voyage into the stratosphere (at an altitude of 60 miles) less than two weeks after the initial exercise, and duly received the $10m X-Prize for the first private spaceship in history.

The sending on this flight of a handwritten note by Jules Verne was a highly symbolic act. Not only is the novelist without any doubt the person who has done most to inspire space travel, but he was also the first to envisage it as a private venture. It was the Gun Club, a private group, that financed the famous rocket to the moon in his *De la Terre à la Lune* (1864) with the backing of a number of businesses independent of government, including the Lombard Odier bank in Geneva.

Additionally Steve Fossett has recently completed a project which has again paid homage to Jules Verne: on 4 March 2005 he achieved a round-the-world journey in less than 80 hours, in a plane, single-handed, in the GlobalFlyer, conceived by Burt Rutan, creator of SpaceShipOne.

The first version of K.P. Rice's Volante, on one of its 300 successful flights.

The second version of the Volante, which was completed in 2003.

Once on the ground, the 'flight' parts of the Rice Volante II were unbolted and towed behind the fuselage, which could then serve as a regular car.

The first patent involving a 'Canard' configuration was applied for in 1989 by Gary M. Bullard, under the description 'Combination Automobile and Airplane'. It was a two-seater with a relatively long fuselage. The main rear-mounted wing folded, but the secondary rear wing and the small 'Canard' front wing staying in place as ground-effect aerodynamic aids when the machine was in road trim. In 1992 Bullard began to sell plans for his GB 2000.

Also to adopt the 'Canard' as a starting point was Anthony Pruszenski's 'Ground-Air-Water Craft' – whose principal novelty was a main wing that pivoted around a longitudinal axis. The wheels retracted and an auxiliary electric motor was used in amphibian configuration.

Even if these projects never got off the drawing board, the future largely belonged to this type of machine. A concrete demonstration was the flying car built by Colonel K.P. Rice. With a degree in aeronautical engineering from the MIT, fighter-pilot Rice began working on his Volante at the end of the 1970s and it made its maiden flight in 1983.

Resembling a 'Canard' – only with a three-wheel configuration – it made more than 300 flights before Rice dismantled it to make a new and improved model. Tested with success since 2003, it closely followed the principles laid down by Molt Taylor: when being used as a car the wings and tail unit could be towed behind in a trailer. Rice, now retired, hopes soon to be able to sell his creation as a build-it-yourself kit. To achieve even this modest aim he will still, however, have to find investors.

The most recent 'Canard' design, only this time with a folding rear wing, has been the Milner Motors AirCar, in development since 2008. Equipped with four doors and intended to carry four people, so far it has only been tested on the road, and currently seems to be on the back-burner.

The AVE Mizar, a flying car built from a Ford Pinto and bits of Cessna – with disastrous results – is here depicted in the March 1975 issue of *Motor Trend* magazine.

The Corgi Super Junior model of an 'E2009 Aerocar' – a toy produced without licence, but clearly based on the flying car in the film *The Man with the Golden Gun*. It should not be confused with Molt Taylor's various Aerocars.

## Don't try this at home!

One of the most persistent urban legends on the internet is the story of how a highway patrolman in Arizona was surprised to discover a smoking wreckage on the ledge of a cliff 120 feet above a bend in the road. What was astonishing was that it wasn't the remains of a plane but rather of a car. A former air-force sergeant had apparently attached a rocket engine to the roof of his Chevrolet Impala in order to make it go at over 200mph – at which speed it became airborne for something like two miles before ending up piling into the rock-face at high speed.

The story – which keeps cropping up – is well and truly fictitious, to the point where the Arizona police have had to issue a formal denial. But it is true that as with so many ground-breaking inventions, flying cars have tended to remain the preserve of lone eccentrics. A resultant lack of knowledge and resources, not to mention a less than perfect mastery of the technology, has inevitable led to the odd catastrophe. Even if Robert Fulton managed to build one of the most successful hybrid vehicles of the time without having any aeronautical knowledge, this wasn't the case for everybody.

Hence a year before Leland Bryan crashed at the controls of his Bryan III (see Chapter 7), the world of flying cars had its first fatal accident. In 1971 Henry Smolinski and Harold Blake founded Advanced Vehicle Engineers in Van Nuys, California. Their aim was to put on sale a modular machine that Smolinski had invented. This was the AVE Mizar, a device that comprised the rear engine, wings and tail unit of a twin-engined Cessna Skymaster attached to a production Ford Pinto.

The first trials were successful and a potential distributor showed an interest in the project, which was intended to enter production during 1974. Unfortunately on 11 September 1973, in the course of further testing, the aircraft part of the Mizar separated from the rest during take-off. The two pilots thus found themselves in the balmy Californian sky at the wheel of nothing more airworthy than a slightly secondhand Ford Pinto. The project did not survive the resultant death of the two partners.

The flying car that an enemy of James Bond pilots in the 1974 film *The Man with the Golden Gun* bears a strong resemblance to the Mizar. The difference, though, was that the machine took to the air only thanks to cinema special effects. When it comes to the exploits of Her Majesty's best-known secret agent, it is on occasion better to stick to fiction...

Half car, half-helicopter, the DAF-Aeromatic 'allows one to reach no matter what destination by air in a minimum of time' – or so this 1971 publicity calendar for the Dutch car and truck company DAF proclaimed. The artwork is by Charles Burki.

# DAF

DAF FRANCE S.A.
95 SURVILLIERS

DAF-AEROMATIC. Les transports terrestres ont également adopté une forme nouvelle. Grâce à ses rotors, le DAF-Aeromatic permet d'atteindre par les airs n'importe quelle destination en un minimum de temps.

**10.**

# The temptation of vertical take-off

At the beginning of the 1980s traditional flying cars were still struggling to make the transition from the drawing-board to the real world. However, thanks to advances in computer science, a new technological approach was seen as a means of popularising the idea and linking it more closely to the image furnished to the general public through science-fiction.

## The VTOLs

The arrival on a large scale of new technologies, in particular in the world of communication, re-energised the concept of a flying car. The arrival of the Global Positioning System (GPS) was seen as an elegant solution to most of the problems of navigation that made air travel a skill reserved for pilots with a greater or lesser degree of training. Would computer technology allow the man in the street to at last live the dream of Icarus? In the world of flying cars the response was clearly in the affirmative.

At the same time inventors sought to develop projects which were closer to the traditional image of a vehicle of the future, as promised for decades in science-fiction. In other words, a flying car should be able to take off from anywhere – a motorway service area, the roof of a skyscraper, a car park – and not just from an aerodrome.

Vertical-take-off planes (tagged VTOL or Vertical Take-Off and Landing) met that requirement. In the beginning they had been conceived out of a fear of landing strips being bombarded in wartime, thereby preventing fighter-planes from being used. The best-known VTOL aircraft is Britain's Harrier 'jump jet'. But the exorbitant cost of making and using such machines has clearly limited their development. In the world of civil aviation, however, one man has devoted himself ceaselessly to the dream of a VTOL for everyone: Paul Moller.

Paul Moller went for the *Top Gun* look when posing in front of his Skycar M400.

Moller's Skycar M400 in road-going configuration. The machine has never flown with a pilot on board.

## The Skycar of Paul S. Moller

A graduate of McGill University in Canada, Paul S. Moller began a brilliant career as a lecturer in engineering and aeronautics at Davis University in California. He developed an interest in the idea of a lightweight VTOL flying car, and alongside his teaching he worked on numerous prototypes, before leaving the university to devote himself full-time to his passion.

In 1983 he set up Moller International in order to develop the Skycar M200X – a device tested from 1989 onwards and for which patents were filed in 1992. His researches were financed by numerous inventions concerning engines, aircraft and associated technologies which he sold to the US army and to big corporations.

As originally designed, the Skycar consisted of a long fuselage equipped with four nacelles, each one containing two independent Wankel rotary engines and a system of flaps that controlled the output and the direction of the jets of air. Three vertical fins and a horizontal wing completed the silhouette. With three on-board computers, the equipment of the proposed VTOL was as high-tech as its look was futurist.

When the M200X actually emerged – under the name Neuera – it was more like a flying saucer than a car; to a certain extent it was a dusted-down and workable version of the Canadian Avrocar, a circular VTOL device ordered by the US army at the end of the 1950s but which never managed to get more than three feet off the ground, despite a $10m bill for its development. The M200X on the other hand proved its viability with more than 200 low-altitude flights at heights of up to 50 feet, at the beginning of the 1990s. Moller followed this with a machine closer to his original patent, the prototype being finished in 1997; this was the Skycar Volantor M400, a VTOL plane the size of a regular car.

A two-seater Skycar variant, the M200 (left), followed the M400; in the foreground is the M200X.

## Behind Man's Conquest of the Skies . . .
## a Master's Touch in Oil

"Flying Saucer"—experimental military craft today —forerunner of your cloud car of tomorrow . . .

First flight in a heavier-than-air machine—the Wright brothers at Kitty Hawk . . .

First plane over the North Pole, first plane over the South Pole—Admiral Byrd's . . .

First 'round-the-world flight—U. S. Army . . .

Lindbergh's lone eagle flight, nonstop New York to Paris . . .

Coast-to-coast propeller plane speed record . . .

*All* have one thing in common—SOCONY MOBIL'S *master touch* in lubrication.

Good reason! When firsts are in the making—when records are at stake—when schedules must be met —the leaders in aviation look to SOCONY MOBIL.

★　★　★

Wherever there's progress in motion—in your car, your plane, your farm, your factory, your boat, your home—*you, too, can look to the leader for lubrication.*

# SOCONY MOBIL OIL COMPANY, INC.
### LEADER IN LUBRICATION FOR NEARLY A CENTURY

Who could have imagined it? Behind man's conquest of the skies, using a circular flying platform, could be found the Mobil Oil Company – or Socony Mobil as it was called when this advertisement appeared in *National Geographic* in 1956.

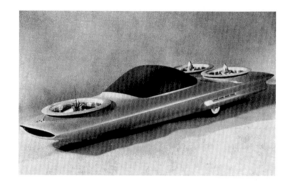

Alex Tremulis, stylist of the famous Tucker, apparently schemed a flying car back in 1944, when he was working for the US Air Force. His concept was close to that of Theodore Hall: a glassfibre body to which one attached a pair of wings, rented at the aerodrome. In 1955, while he was in charge of the Advanced Design section at Ford, Tremulis recruited the young James R. Powers, and had him design futuristic machines as publicity stunts. Among his creations was the atomic-powered Ford Nucleon and 1958's vertical-take-off Ford Volante, as shown here.

SCIENCES et *Avenir*

N° 141 • NOVEMBRE 1958 • REVUE MENSUELLE

PRIX: FRANCE: 120 FR. • BELGIQUE: 20 FR. BEL.

L'aviation commerciale s'apprête à aborder

**l'ère du décollage vertical**

André Franquin was clearly inspired by the Ford Volante when he created the Zorglumobile – here in model form – for the comic book *Z comme Zorglub* (Dupuis, 1962).

A machine combining all the advantages of a rocket and a plane: that was what the November 1958 edition of French magazine *Science et Avenir* imagined, in an issue affirming – somewhat prematurely – that commercial aviation was ready to make the move to vertical take-off.

Capable in theory of reaching a speed of 350mph at an altitude of 30,000ft, the M400 as announced had a more modest claimed cruising speed of 260mph at a stable altitude of 10,000ft, in order to save fuel and to meet legislative requirements. The range was said to be 900 miles, and in order to cope with high-altitude flying the cabin was pressurised.

The power units in the four nacelles together generated 1200bhp – at full power in vertical-thrust mode, this supposedly allowed the Skycar to reach an altitude of 5,000ft metres in 60 seconds. The M400 was conceived to be easy to use: all changes of direction, height and speed were made by controlling the power of each of the eight engines and the angle of the deflector vanes. The machine used petrol, and consumption naturally depended on cruising speed and altitude: in stabilised flight it was claimed to return at least 20mpg but it was thirstier in take-off and when climbing to operating height.

During development a continual emphasis was said to have been placed on safety. It was claimed that the Skycar could take off with just three of the nacelles operational and could continue to fly and land safely with half its engines out of use. There was no feature whose failure would lead to a catastrophe – as for example the principal rotor of a helicopter. Finally the M400 would be equipped with high-tech radar and its manoeuvrability would allow it to avoid any problem, whether as a result of sudden turbulence or when negotiating high buildings or electricity pylons. Needless to say, all this was merely what was claimed in the brochure, which also took care to explain that parachutes were provided for the passengers in the eventuality that something really did go badly wrong.

On 26 October 2002, Paul Moller gave a progress report on his work at the AGM of his shareholders; the M400 lifted off to a height of a few feet, but remained tethered to the ground for alleged safety reasons.

Additionally the M400 would make very little noise. On take-off and landing it would generate 70 decibels at 50 feet – equivalent to the noise made by a passing lorry. That would make it perfectly usable in town, conjuring up that old dream of a future where the roofs of buildings formed landing pads for flotillas of flying machines.

If you compared the M400 to other machines in the same class, such as the McDonnell Douglas 520N helicopter or a small plane such as the EADS Socata TBM-700, its claimed performance was of course superior in all the key areas such as the space needed for take-off and landing, cruising speed, maximum altitude, time to reach operating altitude, and so on. It was only in terms of its quoted fuel consumption that the M400 lagged behind – but future prototypes were spoken of as being able to operate on natural gas or – eventually – on hydrogen, which would considerably lower running costs.

Moller envisaged other Skycar derivatives, carrying model numbers that corresponded to the number of passengers carried: the M150 for one person and the M200 and the M600 for respectively two and six people. He has also studied a version of the M400 in which the nacelles will be mounted on folding wings, thereby creating a modular version of the Skycar which will be more easily parked in a domestic garage.

Even if the Skycar is a long way from being put on sale, products linked to it are already on the shelves, such as this scale model by Sunnyside Ltd.

The retro-futurist style of Torres is particularly delightful when depicting a flying car in *Les aventures sidérales de Rocco Vargas*, as published in 1978 by Casterman.

## A memory of the future?

All this remained pretty theoretic. Tests of the M400 are still in progress, and if Paul Moller is trying to convince his shareholders – through very media-savvy demonstrations – that he is on the right track, at the present time the M400 hasn't got further than 40ft off the ground, and this was without a pilot on board, and with the machine permanently tethered by a safety cable. The revolution in personal transport that Moller is proclaiming seems a long way away, even after the announcement that the company has spent $100m developing the Skycar.

In any case, the M400 has never been billed as a 'flying car'. The four driven wheels of the machine are intended solely to allow it to reach a parking place or an airstrip, and certainly not for urban or motorway traffic. The M400 is not supposed to exceed 40mph on the road: it has been presented above all as a flying machine that forms part of a global vision of society. To have swarms of Skycars taking off and landing, there will need to be numerous places where such vehicles can operate, as opposed to their being limited to aerodromes, as today. The problems are not just technical and financial but also legal, because as things are at the moment you would need a pilot's licence to operate a Skycar. Of course, the latest guidance systems could make the machine entirely automated. You would be a passenger, and not a driver: after having told

The Skycar M400, if it ever makes it to sale, will be available in several versions, such as this police patrol vehicle.

*"This thing couldn't have flown ... ?" I looked at Dialta Downes.*
*"Oh, no, quite impossible, even with those twelve giant props; but they loved the look, don't you see? New York to London in less than two days, first-class dining rooms, private cabins, sun decks, dancing to jazz in the evening ... The designers were populists, you see; they were trying to give the public what it wanted. What the public wanted was the future."*

William Gibson, The Gernsback Continuum, *1981.*

A cover by G. Kaye for *Tom Swift et son Cycloplane* by Victor Appleton II (Grasset, in the series Lecture et loisir, 1957).

the on-board computer where you want to go, the system would look after getting you there, avoiding any other Skycars and keeping clear of other civilian and military air traffic. Just as in the films...

Initially, though, only a limited number of machines would be available – principally to convince new investors, and for military use. There would then be the question of getting the necessary permits from the Federal Aviation Administration. Furthermore, if it does manage to make it to production, the Skycar will remain expensive. If reaches limited production (say 500 a year) then Moller estimates that it will cost half a million dollars a time, or the same as a helicopter or private plane of the same size. In order to bring the price down to that of a top-of-range car, it will evidently be necessary for the Skycar to become an everyday consumer good, or something approaching this.

So even if it were to end up being made in quantity, the cost would probably make its usage above all semi-collective. Its purchase, maintenance and the regular updating of its on-board technology would be more easily taken up by local authorities, private companies or public-transport companies than by even wealthy private individuals. Such a pattern of use would mean that the Skycar could make individual and collective travel easier, over short and medium distances. According to Moller, a number of normal cars could thereby be replaced by a single Skycar – if, that is, the Americans could be persuaded one day to accept the idea of shared travel.

Moller proposes that interested parties reserve a machine by putting down a deposit of between $10,000 and $100,000, depending on how far up the waiting list he or she wants to be; a hundred people are said to have already signed up. On 31 January 2003 the company put the prototype M400 up for sale on eBay, but so far without a customer materialising. Rather more successful at finding a buyer has been the rival Sky Commuter, developed in the 1980s by Boeing: the sole prototype was sold through the on-line auction site in 2008, for more than $130,000.

What all this amounts to is that Moller will need plenty of time to see to fruition a project he began 40 years ago. The fear of not seeing his dream become a reality – or else reading too much science-fiction when he was a youngster – have thus led him to develop an interest in extending the duration of one's life. He has become involved in growing almonds, claiming that almond butter, which he eats regularly, has extraordinary properties. Perhaps these will allow him to live long enough to see his dreams become a reality...

Whether he succeeds or not, Paul S. Moller seems to have become the Molt Taylor of our times, in that he has brought the idea of a flying car back into the public eye. The retro-futurist look of the machine has almost certainly added to the media impact of the Skycar. The

Closer to the imagery of the 1940s than the 21st century? An illustration of the Skycar M400 frequently used by Moller in his advertising.

M400 comes across as a cartoon vision of a certain modernity, like the machines of the future dreamt of by our parents. It is no doubt not an accident that one of the most widespread images of the Skycar is not a photo or computer-generated artwork, but a drawing which seems to have come straight from a 1930s or 1940s pulp comic, one of those cheapskate magazines printed on trashy paper and intended mainly for an adolescent readership.

## The great wave of VTOLs

At the beginning of this third millennium, more than 15 VTOLs are supposedly at one stage or another of research, development or even pre-commercialisation. Even if they don't exist in reality, you can place an order for certain models, with a view to helping their passage into the real world. The companies behind these ventures are all working on broadly similar projects, even if they all maintain that they have of course invented totally new techniques and concepts.

One such project was announced at the end of the 1990s by Macro Industries, based at Huntsville in Alabama. Even if the firm denied being inspired by Moller's work, Macro's SkyRider X2R with its four swivelling turbines had what had become the classic design for a VTOL machine.

Computer-generated artwork showing the Macro Industries SkyRider. The project is still on the drawing board.

It supposedly benefited from all the latest technological advances in aerodynamics, composite materials, control systems and power units, and in line with the most avant-garde dreams of 1950s sci-fi authors was said to represent a revolution in our way of looking at personal transport.

You be the judge: spoken of as being capable of exceeding 300mph, the SkyRider would offer better manoeuvrability than a helicopter, despite its VTOL configuration. Its interior design would be like that of a two-seater sports car, with five-seater and seven-seater versions in prospect. To use it no doubt a special licence would be required, but piloting would be supremely simple. The pilot would gets in, start up, and key in the address or the telephone number for his destination – and the SkyRider would do the rest. If despite all this automation you wanted to switch to the semi-manual mode, then all you would have to do would be to speak to the wonder-machine, since everything would be done with the help of voice-activated controls.

Of course, all this was – and would remain – in the conditional tense: no prototype of the SkyRider has ever seen the light of day...

This *Popular Mechanics* artwork for the SkyRider, from February 2001, recycles the age-old idea of a flying car in every garage...

The car with anti-gravity wheels in *Nick Fury, Agent of Shield*, in the March 1969 issue of *Marvel* (Vol.1 no.10).

Among the other more advanced concepts – or those appearing better adapted to current-day needs – is the X-Hawk (also known as the CityHawk), a modestly-sized platform with two individual cabins one each side of a large central turbine. Schemed in Israel by Dr Rafi Yoeli of Urban Aeronautics, the X-Hawk is principally intended for urban or short-distance use, as an airborne ambulance for example. Even if the X-Hawk is still at an early stage of development, an un-piloted version, the AirMule, has nonetheless made over 40 test flights. One could equally mention Kestrel Aerospace Ltd, one of the more recent companies in this domain. Set up in September 2003 in England, Kestrel is developing versions of a VTOL machine for one to three passengers.

The idea of a one-person machine is not new. In 1998 Wolfgang Ott of the University of San Jose presented his HELIos to the World Aviation Congress at Anaheim, California. It was a vertical-take-off design – and like Moller's Skycar required no modification to switch from road-going to airborne mode. The insect-like design was wildly futurist. It comprised a horizontal ring of 8ft diameter endowed with three spars ending in wheels, two to the front and one at the rear. This ring – more precisely a segment of a cylinder – was at the same time an external fairing housing a pair of co-axial three-blade propellers and an air-retaining suction skirt. Above this and in a forward position was a cabin with a large cockpit equipped with the various controls.

The fuel tank was under the cabin and the engines behind the cabin, which would bring the centre of gravity to a position above the axis of the propellers. Using contra-rotation would eliminate he need for a vertical rear blade. On the road the rear wheel of the HELIos would take the drive, and the controls for road and flight uses would be totally

Trek Aerospace's Springtail EFV-48, photographed in March 2005, is a VTOL backpack for one person.

The cover of *Les aventuriers d'aujourd'hui* no.85, for August 1941, shows hero Brick Bratford equipped with a jetpack (a jet-powered backpack), a means of personal locomotion frequently cropping up in science-fiction.

independent. In aircraft mode the HELIos would use a 179bhp power unit, which allowed its creator to announce a maximum speed of 105mph at a height of 6,500 feet.

Equipped with a seatbelt, an airbag and a parachute in case of mechanical difficulties in flight, as well as a sat-nav system and stabilisation by gyroscope, the HELIos played the card of safety and ease of use; as such it fitted in perfectly with the trends of the time.

Several other would-be constructors focused on one-man vehicles, loosely along the lines of one-man helicopters or flying motorcycles: this was the case with the Springtail and the Dragonfly of Trek Aerospace, the Hummingbird (AD&D, Israel), the airbike of Allied Aerotechnics, Pat Yearic's Cycle-Plane, Charles Medlock's HoverCopter, the Sarus (Aerocopter) from VTOL (Roadable Aircraft Inc), Stefan Hager's FlyRider, John Pirtle's North American VTOL, Michael Aguilar's XplorAir, and the Airscooter – the last a creation of inventor Elwood Norris, already holder of 50 or so patents and recipient of a half-million-dollar prize for one of his projects.

The Skywalker of Mirror Image Aerospace has unfortunately no relationship to the Cloud Cars of Cloud City or the air-taxis of Coruscant which can be admired in certain episodes of the George Lucas series of *Star Wars* films. Planned to be sold as a DIY kit, it is a single-seater VTOL design at a relatively early stage in its development and currently existing only as a quarter-scale model. If the financial means to develop it don't seem evident, at least the 3D modellings are well executed...

In fact, as might be guessed by the camped-up names of the firms studying them, most of these VTOLs exist only as computer-generated images, and their performance is every bit as virtual. Frequently projects of this sort disappear almost at birth, having succeeded merely in generating passing interest in the genre – examples being the Xantus, the K007 Convertiplane of Kulikov Aircraft, and the designs presented by Roadable Aircraft International and AMV Aircraft.

The Cellcraft, conceived by Italian designer Gino d'Ignazio, at least has the merit of being largely an intellectual exercise: the latest in a long series of models along the same lines as Moller's work, it stands out for its elegant lines, but the inventor doesn't hide the fact that he is an illustrator above all, and not an engineer. Despite this, he attracted the attention of Performance Aviation Manufacturing (PAM) of Virginia, which asked him to make their Individual Lifting Vehicle more attractive while they busied themselves with trying to get it off the ground. PAM's ambitions were relatively modest: the cruising speed of the ILV would be about 40mph with a range of roughly 25 miles. Principal uses would be limited to surveillance, aerial photography, agriculture, entertainment or life-saving – just as, in the same style, but on a larger scale, the Eagle of DM AeroPlatforms. The ILV would be as easy to use as a motorcycle,

The VTOL of Kestrel Aerospace Ltd, one of the most recent vertical-take-off projects.

The Skywalker, a personal VTOL machine currently still at the stage of a quarter-scale model.

Two versions of Gino d'Ignazio's Cellcraft, a vehicle equipped with four swivelling jet nacelles to enable vertical take-off.

Allied Aerotechnics don't seem to have got beyond this computer-generated artwork for their Airbike.

Two models of single-person flying platforms developed by Gino d'Ignazio's Performance Aviation Manufacturing, including one designed for fire-fighting.

Among the numerous airborne private vehicles in George Lucas's *Star Wars* series, the most plush is Jabba's anti-gravity barge in 1983's *Return of the Jedi*.

changing direction with the movement of the pilot's body. To be sold for $50,000 in kit form, it was seen as requiring 250 hours of home-assembly before being able to take to the air.

Whatever the seriousness of these projects, the profusion of studies involving vertical take-off arguably shows the correctness of Paul Moller's judgement.

In spite of their often futurist appearance, a question has to be asked concerning the majority of these designs: are they still related to the idea of a flying car? Are they really intended to be used as a car on the road or in town, and at the same time in the air for longer journeys? In the strict sense, the answer is probably no.

As with the helicopter, these VTOL machines are quite simply a different type of vehicle, whether in relation to planes or in relation to cars. What is being proposed is a new non-hybrid approach, made possible – perhaps not straightaway – by today's new technologies. These should allow these machines to take off from anywhere and to avoid collisions even in an airspace filled not only by other machines but also by taller buildings.

The Skycar and the SkyRider are part of a different approach to private flying vehicles. They are means of transport intended in the first instance for town use and over relatively short distances. They would operate in conditions similar to those of the flying cars in Luc Besson's film *The Fifth Element* or the vehicles of the Jetsons, in the famous Hanna-Barbera cartoon series.

The widespread use of VTOLs would entail turning our way of life on its head, along with our town-planning and thereby our social organisation – and this far more radically than would have been the case if the Airphibian, the Arrowbile or the Aerocar had been commercially successful. In this way, perhaps, they herald a future such as that imagined by the science-fiction writers, artists and film-makers of the past.

A model of the Hiller flying car intended for surveillance, depicted on the cover of *Science et Vie* for May 1958, contrasts with the Hiller Aerial Sedan – complete with four horizontal propulsion units – shown on the front of July 1957's *Popular Mechanics* magazine.

**The Hiller Aerial Sedan**

The principle of vertical take-off as a means of propelling a private flying car was explored long before Paul Moller and his Skycar. It was in 1957 that Chrysler and Hiller unveiled the Hiller Aerial Sedan to the press, speaking of production being possible within ten years. With a spacious and comfortable passenger compartment, the Aerial Sedan featured four rotors recessed one into each corner of the body behind chromed slats. The rotors were powered by four petrol engines. This first vertical-take-off flying 'car' had four landing skids and a fold-up step that was operated automatically when the doors opened or closed.

The idea of using horizontal rotors for a civilian vehicle came from the single-seater flying platform Hiller Helicopters had developed for the US Army at the beginning of the 1950s, but which had been little used. The Aerial Sedan was supposed to have the utmost simplicity of operation: once the driver had taken his place a push-button under the steering-wheel would have started the turbines, a lever on the left controlling power (and thus altitude) and a lever on the right the angle of inclination of the nose (and thus horizontal progress). The envisaged cruising speed was 50mph and the price for the four-seater version would be the same as a mid-line motor car.

Two military versions of the Aerial Sedan were also mooted. The Flying Jeep carried over the basic specification of the civilian machine – size, rectangular shape, four-seat configuration, four-rotor power – but more perfunctory trim meant a gain in weight and better airborne performance, in the order of 60mph. As for the Recon Car, this was seen as a two-seat all-terrain reconnaissance vehicle, equipped with only two rotors. A civilian version of the Recon Car was envisaged. This could have been employed by journalists to furnish traffic reports from the sky – bearing in mind that an Aerocar was put to exactly this use.

Whether it was a publicity stunt or a serious venture nipped in the bud, the Aerial Sedan made it to the cover of various magazines before being filed away in the 'Abandoned Projects' pigeon-hole.

Paris-London in a sky-taxi – that was what you could expect in 1968! Here in a late 1958 issue *Meccano Magazine* has picked up on the artwork used a few months earlier in *Popular Mechanics*.

The design of Kenneth Wernicke's Aircar (here seen in 1994 as a full-size mock-up) was certainly original: the machine did not need to be converted from road-going to air-going mode or vice-versa. In theory its very short wings would nonetheless allow it to take off, while keeping width down to a mere 2.6m – meaning it could fit into a standard-sized parking space.

**11.**

## The return of the old favourites

While Paul Moller and so many others did their utmost to get their machines to take off vertically, the dream of a technologically more advanced but still traditional flying car remained alive. Whether conceived by hobbyists – with their head screwed on to a greater or lesser degree – or by aeronautical companies, the classic 'roadable aircraft' hadn't breathed its last, even if sometimes it had to be satisfied with more modest ambitions.

## The push-button principle

By the end of the 1990s all-in-one machines seemed to have returned to favour, but thanks to technological developments there was a move towards an automatic process of conversion. The era when you had to leave your vehicle to add an aircraft section or to fold the wings was over. For simplicity of use the conversion of these new models followed the push-button principle: by operating a simple control in the cabin, the wings unfolded and allowed the machine to take to the air. Some of the technology was a little crude, but that was academic, as most of this new generation of hybrids never left the drawing board.

A figure in the small world of the flying car, German-born Branko Sarh has a degree in automotive and aeronautical engineering from the Massachussetts Institute of Technology. He was an engineer at McDonnell Douglas Aerospace at Long Beach, in California, when in 1991 he applied for a patent for a 'Convertible Fixed-Wing Aircraft' and then created the Advanced Flying Automobile Company, to develop the Sokol A400.

His approach was certainly original. Above all, Sarh felt that the car element should be at the heart of every dual-purpose machine – if only because for most people that would be the most used element. A flying car was above all a car, and so the car part should be as attractive as possible. To achieve his ends – to get off the ground in a vehicle that was comfortable and thus of a certain size – Sarh specified the use of composite materials, these being both strong and light. The main technical novelty, meanwhile, was the telescopic wings that folded out from either side of the vehicle.

Even if his project seems to have stayed on his computer screen, Branko Sarh has been in the vanguard of the movement in organising conferences, principally through the Experimental Aircraft Association (EAA), so key researchers can deliver papers and exchange ideas in a structured fashion.

Mitch LaBiche, with his LaBiche Aerospace Flying Sports Car-1 (FSC-1), adopted the same principle as Branko Sarh, and felt that it was necessary above all to have a road-going element of the highest quality. In the case of LaBiche it was a question of using an existing top-of-range sports car such as a Jaguar XJ220 or Porsche 930. The wings would be folded under the car, which would be raised on hydraulic rams when they were in use, whilst a prop appeared at the rear. The ensemble could be sold as a kit for $175,000, predicted LaBiche.

As for Richard Allen Strong of Dayton, Ohio, he didn't stop with the building of a full-scale model of his Magic Dragon Aircar, a car which automatically converted into a plane, as if by magic. He also founded The Air-Car Research Association (TACRA) in another bid to bring together all those like him who were working on such machines. As for magic, that remained in the hands of magicians, as Harry Potter could vouchsafe when at the beginning of *Harry Potter and the Chamber of Secrets* he uses a Ford Anglia to travel through the air.

Associations such as those of Sahr and Strong could be useful, because one day there will be a need to make a rational assessment of the multitude of projects for dual-purpose vehicles. An eye-catching internet site boasting of the sale 'within one or two years' of such-and-such a machine is far from being an indication of the seriousness of certain projects. Take, for example, the TAERO 4000 of Dr Douglas Ikeler, qualified not in aeronautical engineering but as a vet, and the founder in 2002 of Denver-based Aerospectives, in the same city where he was better known for having set up several hospitals for cats. The TAERO 4000 was supposed to be a revolution in transport. Its single wing pivoted on the roof of what was in appearance a sports car, so that it was parallel to the body when in road-going format, but the technology used was still 'secret' – which was another way of saying that nobody had the slightest idea of how it might or might not work.

As for the Synergy, from Aeromaster Innovations, this seems to have been a work-in-progress for some time, given that a patent was applied for as long ago as 2000 by designer Jeff Spitzer. It was less ambitious, being a small four-seat aircraft with a dual-boom tail and a tailplane with twin fins which gave it the look of a miniature version of the French military transporter the Noraltas; the wings folded vertically either side of the cabin using a hydraulic system, all fully automatic, of course. Having worked for several years alongside Paul Moller on the Skycar M400, he surely appreciated the difficulties of creating a hybrid machine – the reason for which, no doubt, he favoured a more traditional approach.

Robin Haynes at least had the merit of not announcing that his Skyblazer would be fully developed 'by next year'. An industrial designer active for a number of years in the world of aeronautics, he probably knew it would be necessary to be patient if he hoped one day to see his machine fly.

At the beginning of the 2002 Chris Columbus film *Harry Potter and the Chamber of Secrets*, the young wizard makes his escape through the skies at the wheel of a Ford Anglia saloon.

Computer-generated artwork from 2001 depicting the 'Flying Sports Car' of Mitch LaBiche.

With his Synergy, Jeff Spitzer, formerly with Moller International, came up with a more conventional all-in-one design.

A mix of science and magic, the 1997 re-make of Walt Disney's *The Absent-Minded Professor* used a '63 Ford Thunderbird instead of the Model T used in the original film.

Everything is automatic on the proposed Haynes Skyblazer: press a button and the car changes into a plane. Its designer, Robin Haynes, has majored on the safety, comfort and aesthetic apects of the machine.

The list is in fact endless, if you enumerate all those hobbyists, students and engineers, competent or otherwise, who have thought up machines, often with faintly ludicrous names evoking the notion of a hybrid. Such exercises included the AviAuto (Harvey Miller, supported by the Florida Institute of Technology), the ExCitation (Roger Pham), the Fusion Vindicator (Steve Nichols), the telescopic-wing Pegasus (Virginia Polytechnic Institute), the Gregory (George Gregory), the Aircar UK (Gary Payne), the Cane (Matt Fletcher), the CarNard (Palmer Stiles), or more simply the Roadable (Bill Snead, Mark Kettering and Daniel Biezad at Caltech), the Caravellair (Joe Caravella Jr) or the Switchblade (Samson Motorworks).

### Traditional approaches

Whilst all these projects seem to have stalled, without ever getting beyond the stage of a scale model or computer-generated artwork, some studies have tried, more seriously, perhaps, to develop a flying car by building on knowledge acquired in the past, rather than wanting at all costs to start anew.

Thus in 1997 at the World Aviation Congress at Anaheim in California, Dr Steven C. Crow, a graduate of Caltech, presented his StarCar 4. This three-wheeled single-seater would benefit from the status of a motorcycle when on the ground, as had the Arrowbile in times past. In road-going format the wings were fixed either side of the fuselage, into which it sufficed to slot them to move to airborne configuration; they then gave a wingspan of 8 metres. Most of the controls of this simple machine were designed to serve for both modes of travel. The propeller was at the rear

The TAS 102 Flying Motorcycle of Trans Air Systems in a 1998 illustration; the machine is a cross between a motorcycle and a 'Canard'-type plane.

160

LANCE GUEST · DAN O'HERLIHY · CATHERINE MARY STEWART
und ROBERT PRESTON als CENTAURI

## STARFIGHT

Ein Film von NICK CASTLE
Eine UNIVERSAL/LORIMAR Produktion im Verleih der SCOTIA

of the narrow fuselage and was driven by an 1800cc Subaru flat-four. The designer announced a speed in the air of 150mph, with take-off being achieved at 70mph. The StarCar was supposed to be built during 1999 and its first flight was set for 1 January 2000. It was intended to be sold as a modestly-priced build-it-yourself kit, as with most of the models under study in recent years. So everything was thought through...but we're still waiting. The only thing that is certain is that the StarCar was so called in reference to the sci-fi film The Last Starfighter, in which the hero uses a machine of that name to travel in space. We're still a long way from that.

As for the TAS 102 Flying Motorcycle of Trans Air Systems, this consisted of an airborne motorcycle looking a bit like a Waldo Waterman Aerobile to which a 'Canard' front wing had been added. On the road the TAS 102 would use a normal motorcycle power unit, whilst in flight an additional engine would be used, operating a rear-mounted propeller.

The modular Roadrunner of Roger Williamson was another not to sign up to the all-automatic school of thought: it was a three-wheel car that became an aircraft cabin by sliding rearwards inside a fuselage equipped with two wings and landing gear. On the road the wings folded either side of the tail and the rest of the aircraft part was towed. Nothing new under the sun...

The 1984 Nick Castle film *The Last Starfighter* is a riot of teenage fantasies. Not only is the young hero chosen by extra-terrestials to come to their help because he is a champion video-games player, but he leaves Earth aboard the StarCar, a flying car that can also be used in space.

Another 1994 shot of Ken Wernicke's full-scale Aircar mock-up. A lack of funds meant that the machine – seemingly inspired by William Horton's 1951 Wingless Plane – never advanced beyond this stage.

Of the most recent batch of projects, Kenneth Wernicke's Aircar of the early 1990s has genuinely seen the light of day, although it hasn't yet flown. With his Texas-based company Sky Technologies, former Bell Helicopters engineer Wernicke developed a concept that combined the basic principles of a VTOL machine and those of more traditional hybrid machines: the Aircar had no need to be converted, and took off in conventional fashion. The design was very elegant, with a fuselage recalling 1950s cars. At the rear there were three tailfins, at the front the propeller, and the real novelty was in the ultra-short wings, which dropped vertically to form an inverted 'L' halfway along their length. With a resultant wingspan of only 2.6m – height was 2.1m and length 6.6m – the machine could park anywhere. Entirely made of glassfibre, the Aircar had a relatively modest weight and in spite of its slightly oddball looks Wernicke had high hopes for his invention: radio-controlled scale models flew. But he estimated he would need more than $3m to cover research and development costs before he could test a full-scale prototype in flight. Unable to raise such sums, he had to abandon the project.

**The French way: the ultra-light**

Flying cars have tended to be an almost exclusively American pheno-menon, their creation given an important impetus by the sheer distan-ces involved in crossing the country. But projects have been originated other countries lately, even if this remains relatively rare. One such machine is the 'roadable aircraft' presented at the 2004 World Aviation Congress in Reno, Nevada, by Madoka Nakajima of the Japan's Kanazawa Institute of Technology; another is the Autocraft 011 of Yuri Krassin, an aerodynamicist living in Moscow. Both designs were in their very ear-liest stages when unveiled.

Many projects should be regarded with a quizzical eye. Take, for instance, the Triphibian Flying Car announced in 1997 by Zsolt Eugenio Geza Follmann and Adilson Marques da Cunha, of the Instituto Technólogico de Aeronautica in São Paulo, Brazil. According to its creators this machine was destined to become nothing less than the everyday vehicle of the man in the street. It was a comfortable four-seater car, it flew and was amphibious, and was capable of taking off and landing over very short distances, as well as of course being extremely safe and being equipped with automatic driving and navigation systems. 'In bad weather, when most private planes are grounded, taking to the road becomes essential, just as it is for smaller journeys,' stated the publicity, fairly enough. If you weren't totally convinced by the attributes of this giant egg-on-wheels with its backward-looking 1950s lines, perhaps the clincher might be the claim that it 'would save numerous people from premature heart disease due to stress generated by traffic jams on motorways'...

You couldn't get further from such futurist noodlings than the delta-wing flying car of Frenchman Roland Magallon. No nonsense about vertical take-off and landing, no on-board information systems, no costly systems with jet engines and deflector vanes: here we're back in DIY country. See the machine on the road and you'd think it were some sort of beach buggy with a sailboard or a hang-glider fixed to its roll-cage. In fact the load being carried is a delta wing and it is indeed fixed to the vehicle. Ten minutes are all that's needed to unfold it, and then all you have to do is press the accelerator pedal and the car takes flight.

Operational since the end of 2000, Magallon's machine consists of a lightweight body, two forms of propulsion, one for the road, one for the air, two driving systems, and suspension specially adapted for landing and take-off. To this ensemble is added the flexible delta wing, pilotable in hang-glider fashion, and with a transverse spar in carbon-fibre, as used on high-quality sailing boats. Rolled up lengthways, the wing has a length of 3.5m (11ft 6in), so it takes up no more space on the road than an ordinary car.

The machine is flown in an intuitive way by a second steering wheel turned in the desired direction, and which is pulled or pushed to climb or descend – variations in altitude being achieved by larger or smaller throttle openings. Learning all this is claimed to be easy, because hang-gliding with a flexible and deformable wing is a very instinctive process. The machine can reach an airborne speed of 100mph and can withstand winds of approaching 40mph. A dog-clutch system similar to that of a 4x4 allows automatic engagement of flight mode with the propeller – placed at the rear between two vertical tail fins – or alternatively road-going mode with the power going to the wheels.

With its contemporary design and 4x4 character, the delta-wing flying car targets the same customer base as that for ultra-lights and light planes. Furthermore, it has potential for delivering important services in countries with a poor road network. At the moment it is still awaiting interest from investors.

Gerry Anderson's 1965 puppets became flesh-and-bones actors in the 2004 big-screen version of *Thunderbirds*, directed by Jonathan Frakes. Lady Penelope's car, FAB1, here shown on a Ford motor-show stand, took to the air solely thanks to special effects.

*The Korean people created the first flying car 400 years ago in order to combat its enemies. This flying car in the form of a bird could accommodate four passengers. It was equipped with machinery to move the wings, but also to store the wind and expel the air as required. It took off using the flexible wings and propulsion provided by the stocked air, and flew by beating and moving the wings. This car made its appearance a good time before 1783, the date when man is regarded as having flown for the first time in a hot-air balloon. According to the master O Myong Ho, researcher at the History Institute at the Academy of Social Sciences, this clearly shows that our Korean ancestors have contributed enormously to the development of aviation. They used flying cars in their battles against foreign aggressors. In 1592, during the Patriotic War of Imjin, a unit of the Korean army in Jinju castle in the province of South Kyongsang was encircled by Japanese troops. The unit therefore had to fly a car over 12km to make contact with another unit. In another instance, in 1374, during the Koryo dynasty (919-1392) soldiers of the Korean army flew balloons off warships as far as the island of Jeju, to secure victure against the Japanese enemy.*

Press release from the Central Information Agency of North Korea, Pyongyang, 11 February 1998.

Summer 1959, and Ed Sweeney was 17 years old. Working in the family plywood business in Longview, Washington, he was a passionate aero-modeller and spent his spare time flying his models at the local aerodrome. From time to time he saw a bizarre machine that a certain Moulton Taylor had developed. That the two should meet was inevitable, and sure enough one day Taylor offered to take the youngster up in one of his Aerocars, N102D.

1988, and many years had passed since that memorable flight. Sweeney had remained as keen as ever on his childhood hobbies and had become editor of American *Aircraft Modeller and RC Sportsman*. Not only did he collect planes but he also loved cars and had four Lotuses. One day his son Eric saw a small ad for a Messerschmitt 109 in *Trade-a-Plane*. He showed the ad to his father, who already had a Messerschmitt 209. Sweeney had a look at the paper...and nearly fell off his seat. Beside the ad for the Messerschmitt there was another for a much more interesting plane: someone was offering an Aerocar for sale. The next day Sweeney set off to Florida to see the vendor. He returned two weeks later with a job-lot of parts amongst which was a complete Aerocar. By a quirk of fate it was N102D, the very same machine in which Moulton Taylor had taken him up almost 30 years earlier.

Sweeney started to trace its history. The first 'customer' Aerocar, it had been sold to Bob Cummings and had appeared many times in his TV programme, in the colours of show sponsor Nutrabio. In February 1962 Cummings had sold N102D, and from 1965 the machine was passed from pillar to post, having at least three different owners who scarcely used it. The last owner employed it as a crowd-puller at supermarket openings.

Dismantled, rebuilt and painted anew in Nutrabio's yellow and green livery, Aerocar N102D is again participating in airshows, and attracting the same attention as in the past. But Sweeney has done more than merely buy an Aerocar: he has literally become the guardian of the flame.

Persuaded that there was still mileage in the idea, he started to work on a prototype, called Aerocar V in homage to Moulton Taylor. For the car element Sweeney wanted to use a high-performance production car, and chose the Lotus Esprit, with its mid-mounted 150bhp engine. This he supplemented with a second engine in the aircraft part of the machine, with the two power units intended to be used together when the Aerocar was in flight. At the end of the 1990s Aerocar V became Aerocar 2000, this time with a front-engined Lotus Elite being mated to a flying part weighing less and having more power.

The idea is to sell the flying element in kit form, to be fitted to an existing road car, which makes the Aerocar 2000 more akin to a vehicle such as the AVE Mizar than to the ideas of Moulton Taylor. There's also the consideration that the aeroplane elements aren't intended to be towed in a trailer and will have to kept on the aerodrome. Only the future will tell if the new Aerocar – which has not yet left the ground – will have as much success as its ancestors built by Molt Taylor.

In the same vein the Americans have come up with the Para-Cycle, a bicycle equipped with a motorised parachute. There's no dual-purpose engine here: on the ground it's your pedal-power that gets you around. The Flite-Bike fortunately remedies this inconvenience, since the roadgoing element is a Honda Reflex motorbike. In flying mode it also uses a Buckeye-type motorised parachute, as invented by Albert J. Bragg, who a few years previously had tried to make a flying car, the Skytrek.

As the history of flying cars is a constant reinvention of the wheel, we should not be astonished by the French Flycar. At the famous Concours Lépine for inventions, in 2005, this picked up the medal awarded by the extravagantly-titled Minister of the Interior, Internal Security and Local Freedoms. Produced by the Adventure firm, it consists of a two-seater car with two wheels at the front and a single wheel at the rear, and flies courtesy a motorised parachute. Maybe the word 'car' is over-stating things: the Flycar is maxed-out at 30mph on the road, and only the fitment of headlamps, a horn and indicators distinguish it from a common-or-garden ultra-light. A similar device, albeit a bit more sophisticated, is the Begalet, created in Russia by Scarab Aviation Labs.

It was with a machine of this nature – albeit with four wheels – that in 2009 a former member of Britain's SAS, Neil Laughton, successfully covered the 6000 or so miles from London to Timbuktu, including flying over the Straits of Gibraltar and the Sahara, in a venture tagged the 'Skycar Expedition'.

Altogether more modest than the VTOLs or the new 'classic' flying cars, such machines might make one smile. However, they represent an interesting alternative vision; more to the point, they actually fly, unlike a number of more ambitious machines. Indeed one has to acknowledge the lack of success of engineers over nigh-on 40 years: apart from traditional hybrids such as the Aerocar (which is still capable of flying), no design has proved to be viable. All the recent machines are a long way away from the performance of the machines of Waterman, Hall and Taylor.

The reason for this failure lies perhaps with the means needed to build a flying car these days, with the new technologies available, and to make it conform with legislation. Given the sums already spent by enthusiasts such as Paul Moller, for the moment without great success, the realisation of the dream of a bi-functional vehicle would seem inevitably compromised for inventors working on their own, working in their domestic garage or, more generally, solely on paper.

New projects for flying cars pop up every year, making the front page of one paper or another, accompanied by computer-generated images that are to a greater or lesser degree attractive. Having briefly been a talking point they then disappear into the mist, leaving behind them pages on the internet announcing the arrival of a flying car in the near future, on sites that end up not being updated for four years.

These companies only foster the myth of the flying car's unfeasibility.

They leave it in the domain of the imagination through the very act of trying to make it a reality, by lacking the means to follow through and create anything concrete. Forever inventing machines that are often more fantastic than anything seen in science-fiction, they fight to be the first in this new field, which would throw the sky open to each and everyone. But unless they are prepared to return to the more simple concepts of 50 years ago, or to adopt a radically different approach, with support from governments, the dual-purpose road they have chosen seems difficult.

### A new white hope: the Terrafugia Transition

Today all eyes are on Terrafugia's Transition. It is far and away the flying car that has been most talked-of these past few years, having re-activated media interest in the breed, as seems to happen every ten years or so.

Based in Massachussets, Terrafugia's 12-strong team has been working on a flying car since 2006, under the leadership of brilliant ex-MIT engineer Carl Dietrich. If the Transition innovates with its use of composites and its on-board information systems, the principles underpinning it are pretty classic: it is an 'all-in-one' machine with wings that fold in and out automatically. Measuring 19ft 9in long, it has a width of 90in in road-going format, a wingspan of 26ft 6in, and can carry two people. It is not a car, and is good for only 65mph on the road, against 115mph (and a range of 490 miles) in the air. To take off or land it needs a runway or a straight stretch of road 1,700 feet long, so in-town take-offs aren't on the menu.

The first trials of the machine proved a success, retired colonel Phil Meeter taking to the air for the first time in March 2009, over Plattsburg, New York State. After a new series of tests, the Transition has now been homologated by the FAA (the Federal Aviation Administration) as a 'Light Sporting Airplane'. All that is needed to fly it is therefore a simple sports-pilot licence, obtainable after a minimum of 20 hours of flying time. In all, 24 customers have already yielded to temptation and placed a $10,000 deposit. Meanwhile a new and more evolved version of the Transition is under study. Whether the 2012 delivery date will be respected is another matter: the history of the flying car teaches one prudence in such matters...

That said, in November 2010 Terrafugia won an important contract with the US Army to develop the Transformer, a four-person machine suitable for road and air use. The $65m programme aims for a conclusive outcome by 2015. With this sort of support, Terrafugia would appear to have a solid future in front of it. Even if this won't result in a car for the average man in the street, thanks to an envisaged price-tag of $200,000 to $250,000, perhaps it will nonetheless find a healthy customer base amongst the moneyed élite. After all, it has a boot big enough to take a set of golf clubs, the brochure tells us...

The Vertiport Metroplex Hub, an urban airport intended
to be served by mid-range versions of the CarterCopter
gyroplane; a 2001 illustration by C. Michael Lewis.

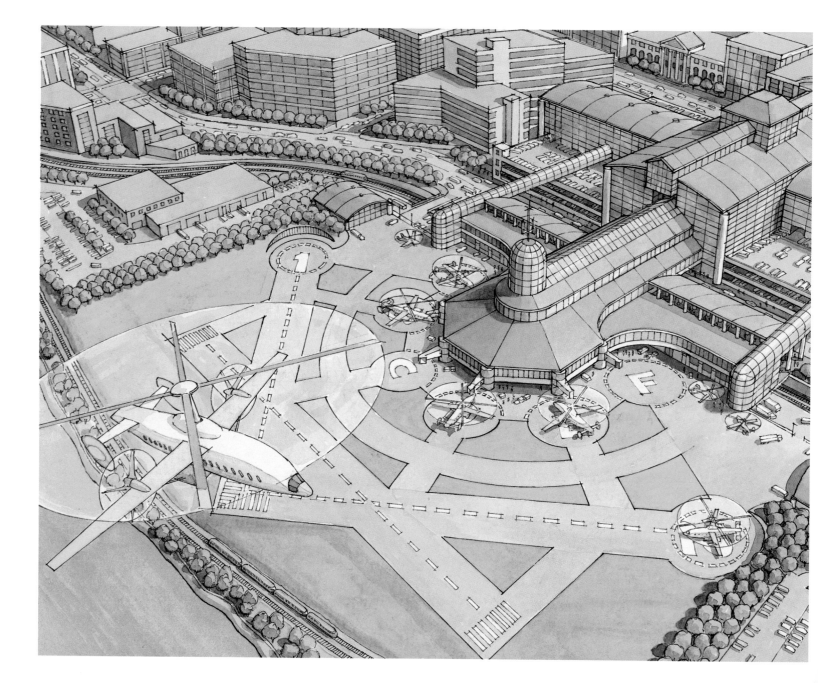

# 12

## Tomorrow – motorways in the sky?

To see the dual-purpose vehicle promised by science-fiction appearing in the workshop of today's average hobbyist would truly be astonishing – and this despite the tenacity and talent of certain inventors. But their efforts have not been in vain. In seeking to extend the limits of our range of everyday travel, in maintaining interest in the fantasy of being able to take to the air whenever you might be stuck in a traffic jam, they have laid down the mould for what is today regarded as a flying car.

## The awakening of the giants

We have recently seen a new phenomenon. Large automobile and aviation concerns have started to show an interest in dual-purpose machines, either feeding the rumour-mill with details of secret projects or even presenting prototypes to the press.

For a long time car manufacturers have occasionally asked artists and illustrators to give free rein to their imagination and create futurist models, to give customers something to dream about or to star at international motor shows. Only rarely have such ventures sprung from a genuine wish to create a new form of locomotion. Sometimes it was simply a way of stimulating the firm's engineers by showing them a possible vision of the future. This was the intention of Harley J. Earl, vice-director of General Motors and the firm's design chief from the end of the 1920s until 1958. He felt that it was necessary to push design concepts beyond what was realisable – or even realistic – because otherwise you would never be able to produce truly revolutionary ideas. Earl therefore set up a department specialising in advanced research, in the full knowledge that even if the concepts that emerged would never see the light of day, they would provoke thought among the firm's researchers.

In the same way Ford unveiled the Ford Volante, one of a number of left-field creations dreamt up by the fertile imagination of designer James Powers. In 1958 photos of this car with its central turbine (which made it a VTOL) were reproduced just about everywhere to promote the marque and its rôle in the great march of progress – even if the Volante never passed the stage of a scale model.

What is happening at the moment seems in some ways similar. In 2005, for example, Mercedes-Benz Advanced Design of North America presented a flying-car concept vehicle in the 'Design Los Angeles' section of the Los Angeles Auto Show. Inspired by the 300SL with its famous gullwing-doors, the 2005 version had four directional turbines to allow vertical take-off. Doubtless this 'Ultimate LA Machine' – as its creators called it – is a bit of thinking aloud, or even an exercise in whimsy, and will remain a drawing and northing more.

Such initiatives are above all PR operations. What is true, however, is that studies are today being carried out by industry giants such as Boeing to come up with alternative solutions to current modes of transport. The way forward was opened up by NASA. It might appear surprising that an American body known principally for its work in the domain of space should interest itself in flying cars, but that is to forget that the 'National Aeronautics and Space Administration' has been behind a number of advances in aeronautics.

## Keeping mobile in the age of mass mobility

Certain NASA programmes since the beginning of the 21st century have sought to respond to a major problem in civil aviation in the States: its hubs (airports connecting different routes) are becoming more and more saturated. At present, 70 per cent of passengers use just the 30 biggest US airports. The principle of centralisation and redistribution ('hub and spoke') is evidently attractive economically for the airlines, because it assures them of a high rate of aircraft occupancy. But this rationalisation penalises many passengers, because rural regions are poorly served and there are serious delays at the principal airports – a situation aggravated by the security measures put in place since the September 11 attacks.

At the same time studies on mobility in the US have shown that for distances of over 90 miles the car is still chosen as means of travel in 75 per cent of cases. That figure is even higher (95 per cent) for journeys of less than 500 miles, and people are still preferring to drive rather than fly even for distances of 900 miles or more. The plane is thus seen as not being sufficiently practical or flexible: after all, one has to conform to the timetable imposed by the airline companies.

However the car has also reached its limits. It is striking to have to state that during the past hundred years the average daily time on the road has not changed: one and a quarter hours. An American might cover more miles per day (50 miles in 2000 against ten in 1900) but he doesn't save any time. On the contrary: in the future he will be taking forever longer on his journeys thanks to over-crowding on the roads. It is estimated that in heavily urbanised areas such as Los Angeles the average speed of 35mph recorded today will drop to 25mph in the next 20 years. That hardly makes it worthwhile to move further away from one's place of work to find peace and quiet and a cheap patch of land...

An air-taxi of the future on the cover of Barbara Slawig's novel *Flugverbot* (Argument Verlag, 2003).

*Even the long-term concept of operations is not daring to imagine the vision of* Star Wars *with aerial vehicles completely replacing autos and blotting the sun in densely populated urban areas.*

*Mark D. Moore, NASA Langley, 2003.*

The 'Escacar Unicycle Gyroscopic Rocket Car' drawn in 1945 by Carl H. Renner for General Motors. It is a single-wheel rocket-car with a name that suggests that it was intended to be able to escape from traffic by taking to the air.

## Personal Air Vehicles

Armed with these observations, Mark D. Moore, a researcher at NASA's Langley centre in Hampton, Virginia, concluded in 2003 that there was a need to react by turning, in due course, to PAVs, or Personal Air vehicles. Initially the term 'converticar' was used, but this was ultimately discarded, presumably because it was felt not serious enough and smelt a bit too much of the world of science-fiction; the word 'flying car' was also avoided, as the symbol of a dream condemned to remain inaccessible.

But the public wasn't going to be bothered by such semantics. Whatever you called the relevant machine, the use of a new system of air transport, based on a non-centralised infrastructure and 'distributed' according to demand, would allow a considerable amount of time to be saved. This isn't all that far removed from the basic idea that the flying-car pioneers had, all those decades ago: minimise car use over long distances, whilst at the same time avoiding spending days waiting around at airports. That's not an unattractive thought, as currently the flight itself represents only 30 per cent of the actual time spent on an air journey, whether for short-hail or medium-length flights.

The novelty of Mark Moore's thinking was that he wasn't talking of replacing the private car or traditional commercial flights, or even gaining time. Rather, the PAVs would allow a supplementary level of services to be offered, principally to extend the daily radius of action of suburb-dwellers. This mobility could be extended to 250 miles, or even 500 miles, per day. The research having been carried out in the US, it has to be observed that the express train, just as other forms of public transport, hardly entered into the equation when it came to considering the impact of transport systems on the countryside.

To make a Personal Airborne Vehicle an everyday form of transport the problems needing to be solved are evidently numerous, as the history of the flying car has shown. Principally, such a machine has to be not only technically feasible but also economically viable. It must therefore have limited production costs, be able to be integrated into existing transport systems (rather than being in competition with them) and be easy enough to be used by the general public and not just by aviation buffs.

The cockpit of a PAV would thus have to resemble that of a car rather than that of an aircraft and the pilot's licence would have to be easier and less expensive to obtain – currently you need to allow $14,000 and several months to obtain an ordinary pilot's licence. The vehicle would need to be largely automatic, so it could detect potential problems before take-off, follow emergency procedures, and provide information on weather conditions and even react in consequence to these. NASA calls this technology the 'H' system – 'H' standing for horse. Just like a horse, a PAV would be able to avoid obstacles and even get its driver home, thereby assuring his safety.

Further to this, the noise emitted is seen as being limited so as not to cause a nuisance to the population – an average of 55dB being deemed acceptable. Knowing the problems faced by those living near airports, it is easy to imagine that the situation would be totally unbearable if the new machines were as noisy as planes of today, seeing as they would be flying in fair numbers over a large part of the territory.

Finally, the infrastructure to support the vehicles could pose a problem. It was necessary to build motorways criss-crossing a large part of the United States, at huge cost, before the car became a truly efficient form of transport. But in the case of the PAVs, an infrastructure is already in place for small planes, and is notably under-utilised: there are at least 14,000 aerodromes and 10,000 heliports. The majority of the American population is therefore less than half an hour away by car from a place that could serve as an air-station.

The era of personal airborne transport in an illustration by Morrow for Keith Laumer's story *The Planet Wreckers*, in February 1967's *Worlds of Tomorrow*.

**Aviation for Everyman**

Initially the NASA researchers envisaged the personal flying machines as belonging to companies who would operate them on behalf of customers. But today low-cost airlines have developed new routes using smaller and cheaper airports, thereby transforming the mobility of travellers. In a near future, all the same, the flexibility of air transport could be further improved by the arrival of PAVs, which would function as airborne limousines – as real air-taxis, piloted by professionals and serving any aerodrome. Companies working on VTOLs, such as Urban Aeronautics or Moller, also imagine this as a first stage, combined with government use by police, customs and hospital services.

Once production costs have dropped sufficiently and PAV use has been simplified, the market could open up to take in machines piloted by the general public. Contrary to the idea of most of those who had worked on flying cars – mostly private individuals working in their garage, or small businesses – NASA envisages that there would be various different types of personal flying vehicle. Just as today there are so many different types of car, from a Smart to a powerful off-roader, so different airborne vehicles would respond to different needs.

The first type of PAV would serve rural areas and the regions around. Much of the population lives far from urban agglomerations and a centralised system of air transport isn't much use to them today. On the other hand, small simple machines using already-existing local aerodromes could integrate these communities into a bigger transport network.

The Tailfan, conceived by the Langley centre, represents to a certain extent the next stage in the evolution of traditional aviation. It is a CTOL vehicle – Conventional Take-Off and Landing – and is designed to be above all cheap, safe and relatively silent, even to the detriment of its performance.

A private flying saucer depicted in the March 1957 issue of *Mechanix Illustrated*: as with the machines envisaged today by NASA, it was seen as making a miniature airport of everyone's back garden. The plastic-bodied flying saucer would allow the honest working man to travel to his place of work, a good 60 miles away, in a mere half-hour. To be sold at the price of an average family car, such a machine could be a reality by 1965, predicted the magazine...

Such, in any case, is the principle behind what has also been given the name EquiPT – short for 'Easy to use, quiet Personal Transportation'.

The fuselage of the Tailfan, built as a stressed aluminium structure, would be manufactured with the utmost simplicity, along car-industry lines. Maximum standardisation would encompass symmetrical framework, reducing the number of different parts to manufacture, and the use of an existing V8 car engine such as that of the Chevrolet Corvette LS-1. This would power a ducted fan rather than a propeller. Even if this made the machine heavier than a small plane, the cost gain would be in the order of 60 per cent: the Corvette LS-1 engine on its own is eight times less expensive than a proper aero engine. With a production of 2000 units per year, the Tailfan would cost around $75,000. It could accommodate four passengers and reach 200mph, with a range of 500 miles. A more potent version of the Tailfan at $125,000 could also see the light of day: it would have a pressurised cabin and a maximum speed of 300mph.

In England, Avcen Ltd worked along the same simplified lines for its Jetpod. This wasn't a private vehicle, being designed above all to serve as on-demand public transport. Its seven passengers would travel for a reasonable sum over short distances – between London airports and the city centre, for example. Suitably quiet and needing only 125 metres to take off – hence the appellation VQSTOL (Very Quiet Take-Off and Landing) – the Jetpod is seen as being particularly suited to urban use.

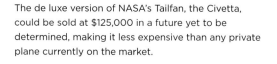

The de luxe version of NASA's Tailfan, the Civetta, could be sold at $125,000 in a future yet to be determined, making it less expensive than any private plane currently on the market.

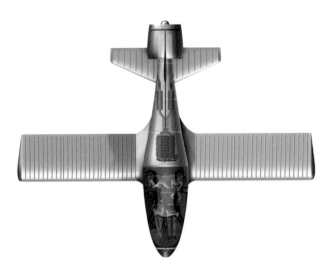

It would reach 35mph and make up to 50 flights per day, thereby functioning as a true air-taxi. With fewer than a hundred such machines, a city could see its road traffic diminish by tens of thousands of journeys daily. With the help of funding from the local authorities in London and from the EU, Avcen claimed that its machine could cost less than a million dollars and could be available in its initial 'customer' version by 2010. But the death of the firm's founder in Malaysia in August 2009, during the fourth test flight of the Jetpod, was a grave blow, and the company has apparently pulled down the shutters.

While aeronautical companies such as Adam Aircraft or Cessna carry on trying to develop ever less expensive planes, car-maker Honda is also working on a project for a small private plane. The Japanese firm, active for some years in the domain of aero engines, has in effect decided to design a small plane in its entirety, following the principle that made it a success in the car industry in the 1970s, notably in the States: a simple, quiet, economical and cheap machine, destined to compete against bigger vehicles using an ageing technology. The Hondajet would transport six passengers at 500mph with a range of 1200 miles.

Officially the Honda aircraft is merely a prototype, and there are no plans to make it. However, when it was announced, Ford also launched a similar programme of research so as not to be outflanked – at least according to internal sources at the company. As these two projects are not only quite recent, but are also protected by industrial secrecy, it is too soon to know what the future holds for them.

Finally one should note the CarterCopter project, developed by Jay Carter Jr and his team (including Ken Wernicke, inventor of the Aircar in the 1990s). An innovatory combination of autogyro and plane, it is therefore a gyroplane: its monoplane wings, narrower in cord than on a traditional plane, only serve a purpose when the plane has reached its cruising speed, whilst the rotor is used principally on take-off and

NASA's Tailfin in its most simple version: it was envisaged as being cheap, easy to use, and quiet in operation, while carrying four passengers. A ducted turbine served as propulsion and the structure was in aluminium.

Avcen Ltd's Jetpod in its air-taxi version: its range was seen as being limited, but it would represent a considerable time-saving for its users, by avoiding particularly difficult traffic in the bigger cities.

The prototype CarterCopter in flight, the gyroplane having been successfully tested since 1998.

landing. The rest of the time it simply idles. Contrary to a helicopter, the CarterCopter cannot maintain a stationary position in the air. However, it can take off and land vertically: with the rotors with their ballasted ends in assisted rotation, the initial thrust is calculated to enable it to attain a height and speed at which it can make the transition from vertical to horizontal flight.

The CarterCopter prototype has already flown several times, and despite certain technical problems has reached an altitude of 9800ft and a speed of 170mph. NASA has recently decided to support the project, principally so a version with folding wings can be developed, suitable for use on the road. At this stage it is not intended to put the machine on the market, Carter being happy to stick to perfecting the design. In the future the idea is to develop a 120-passenger Heliplane Transport version, which would operate from a Vertiport Metroplex Hub (VMH), a city-centre airport intended specifically for these vehicles.

If the initiative seeking to develop an EquiPT vehicle, a Jetpod or a CarterCopter seems far from the idea of a flying car, it demonstrates all the same an interest in new types of more simple and less expensive personal plane. Above all, it stakes out the ground for the eventual appearance of a truly hybrid vehicle.

In fact, NASA's work on the Tailfan seeks not only to bring flying within the reach of everyone but also to change certain legal aspects hampering the arrival of low-cost aircraft. One aspect of this is whether to move from a system of controls on quality to one of assurance of quality. Rather than have every component of every aeroplane certified, as the US administration demands today, with the significant costs this implies, the aim would be rather to have the overall specification approved, as with a motor car.

The other essential point, in order to make this vision a reality, has to be to find a way of controlling a clearly more dense amount of air traffic. At the beginning of the 20th century the population was worried about the proliferation of the motor car. Would one have to have a policeman at every road junction to control the traffic? Nobody dared think what that might cost. But a simple system was put in place, starting in 1912: traffic lights. NASA is therefore working at a means of organising airspace, the SATS or 'Small Aircraft Transportation System'. Conceived in partnership with the federal aeronautical administration and NCAM (the National Center for Advanced Manufacturing), a consortium uniting 130 organisations and six research labs, the project has a sizeable budget of $80m, spread over five years.

SATS is about developing not just new technologies but above all an overall policy to promote personal aviation. The principal aims of the programme are to allow small airports to manage a bigger volume of traffic (above all in bad weather) and to make piloting much simpler. In equipping each machine with on-board computers and satellite navigation, it would be possible to offer the pilot a route he can follow on a screen, as in a video game: the Highway in the Sky. The screens in the cockpit wouldn't only show 3D images for navigation (other aircraft approaching, landing paths, lines of horizon, etc) but also the central information system would function as an automatic anti-collision programme. The plane could thus fly without problem, even in conditions of reduced visibility. This virtual air-traffic controller would spare airports the financially costly construction of a control tower and would make them easily accessible.

SATS, initiated in 2001 and of which the first results were presented in June 2005 at a big meeting at Danville (Virginia), could be introduced in 2015 and be fully operational by 2020.

*'It's times like this it occurs to me that we were lied to by "The Jetsons".'*

*'What are you talking about?'*

*'According to that show we were supposed to be tooling around in flying cars by now. You see any flying cars lately? That's the problem with TV, it always lies to us.'*

*'Yeah, well most of us rational thinkers weren't banking on a cartoon to offer us a viable glimpse into the future of technological development.'*

*Kevin Smith,* The Flying Car *(extract from the short film's script, 2002).*

A computer-generated image of the CarterCopter private plane: certain versions of Jay Carter Jr's creation were intended to be usable on the road.

## A plurality of flying cars

With the development of the Tailfan and the introduction of the 'Highway in the Sky', a hybrid vehicle now seems almost superfluous. In effect, you could drive by car to the airport half an hour from home and jump into a plane that you could drive as easily as your car. You would then fly to your destination, even if it were a distance from any big urban centre, and hire a car on your arrival. What use would there be for an Aerocar of the sort imagined by Molt Taylor?

Happily, NASA hasn't closed the door on that dream. Indeed, the EquiPT machines are only one part of a new system of transport that could be put in place. The second type of PAV currently being studied is an intra-urban vehicle, complementing small private planes and the aircraft of the traditional airlines. With a range of a few hundred miles only, it would be capable of taking off from within a town or city – from public car parks, university campuses, heliports – and rapidly reaching the terminals of airports or shuttling between home and work. These wouldn't be machines you'd have on your driveway, but would be kept a mile or two away, on a supervised airfield. Vertical take-off and landing would not be necessary: in towns it should be possible to build short runways with a length as short as 150 yards. On the other hand, for evident reasons of convenience, it would be important that such vehicles could use the roads – contrary to the Jetpod, for example.

This takes one back to the idea of a flying car. The researchers at the Langley centre thus came up with a hybrid vehicle, the 'dual-mode concept', resembling a sports car equipped with folding wings and a front fin unit of the 'Canard' type. The result wasn't satisfactory: it would be too heavy, too expensive, and too bulky. Furthermore, the NASA engineers had done their homework, and could see that the numerous attempts to create such vehicles had failed, largely because they sought to create a something that was as effective as a car as it was as a plane.

Showing their pragmatism, they stipulated that the road-going performance of the machine could be limited. It wouldn't be a question of competing with a regular car, but merely being able to travel a short distance, at reduced speed (25–30mph) in order to reach a suitable airstrip. The only design criterion was that the width should not exceed 8ft, so that normal roads could be used. The resultant Gridlock Commuter was just such a machine.

This wasn't a VTOL, but rather a STOL ('Short Take-Off and Landing'), capable of taking off in a short distance, about 80 yards, at a speed of only 30mph. Resembling a large turbine on roller-skates, the Gridlock Commuter used SpiralDuct technology (suction in a spiral) inspired in part by the work of Alexander Lippisch, the German engineer and pioneer aerodynamicist 'imported' into the United States after the Second World War. Compact and equipped with an engine of less than

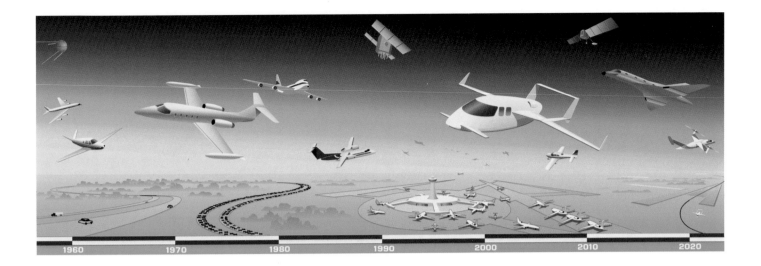

**Possible timetable for Personal Air Vehicles, as proposed by NASA**

2005    Demonstration of Small Aircraft Transportation System (SATS)
2007    Launch of first new-generation private planes, low-cost and quiet
2008    Demonstration of anti-collision programmes
2009    Announcement of new type of simplified cockpit
2011    Certification of single-pilot air-taxis
2012    Introduction of principles of Quality Assurance in aeronautical industry
2013    Installation of first elements of Highway in the Sky
2015    Demonstration of Gridlock Commuter
2016    Simplification of procedures to obtain pilot's licence
2022    Development of first urban take-off pads for Extreme Short Take-Off and
        Landing vehicles (ESTOLs)
2025    Introduction of VTOL air-taxis
2028    Appearance of totally autonomous airborne vehicles
2030    Annual PAV production exceeds 250,000 units, representing 3 per cent of
        the US car market

The past, the present and the future of transport, as seen by NASA in an illustration by Bill Kluge. The Small Aircraft Transportation System was envisaged as helping to unclog the road network, as well as flight 'hubs', and accelerating the use of low-cost planes and small airports.

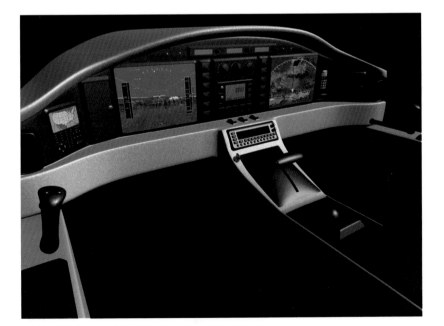

A simplified cockpit is one of the basic requirements for putting air travel within everyone's reach, according to NASA's Langley research centre. Use of computer-generated navigation and information systems could make flying an aircraft almost as easy as driving a car.

A family returns home in its helicopter after a visit to the grand-parents in this 1947 illustration by Alexis V. Lapteff. In all probability Lapteff was influenced by the work of Russian émigré Igor Sikorsky, who predicted in the 1940s that helicopters would soon replace the family car.

An early idea by NASA for a dual-function vehicle, the so-called Dual-Mode Concept. It was deemed to have the failings of both a plane and a car.

100bhp, the machine was supposed to attain 120mph in flight, with a maximum range of 375 miles. After having landed, it would fold its small wings along the ring-shaped fuselage and slot into traffic at the speed of a moped. The only snag – perhaps – was that it would only seat one or two people.

## A shared vision

The development of such vehicles and the establishment of a totally new concept of mobility will take time. NASA has therefore called for rapid decisions. There needs to be advance planning to avoid America finding itself paralysed by overcrowded highways and over-trafficked airports. Furthermore, small aerodromes, thanks to the concentration of the airlines on the bigger airports, are often poorly maintained. They will need to be kept in order, or else they will have to be entirely replaced within 20 or 30 years.

These recommendations cannot of course be carried through without political backing. The role of NASA – a federal body that has amongst its aims economic growth and the improvement of the quality of life of the American citizen – is evidently crucial, but it must be seconded by the private sector. Even if it is too soon today to determine if air transport will take the direction sought by the Agency in the relatively near future, it is certain at least that the industry is starting to become seriously interested. This is the case, as we've seen, for light aircraft, but also for true hybrid vehicles.

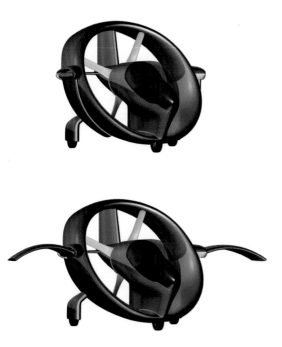

The Gridlock Commuter was seen as being complementary to small low-cost aircraft. The device could travel about town a low speed until a place to take off could be found. It would be able to take off within a short distance, with one or two passengers on board.

The Boeing Personal Air Vehicle, a wheeled twin-rotor helicopter, photographed in model form at Seattle's Museum of Flight, in front of Molt Taylor's Aerocar III.

179

One of the three models of autogyro currently in production at the Magni Gyro works at Besnate, near Milan.

The PALV of 2004, a combined enclosed motorcycle and light aircraft created by Spark Design in the Netherlands, largely as a publicity stunt.

Thus at the same moment as Airbus was developing its flying cruise-liner, the A380, American giant Boeing was displaying its version of a flying car at the Museum of Flight. When one of its managers posed with the model of its personal plane in front of Aerocar III, the Seattle firm clearly associated itself with of the work of Molt Taylor.

Presented as the result of a first feasibility study carried out by engineer Darold Cummings, the vehicle consists of an elegant combination of a three-wheeler car – two wheels at the front, one at the rear – and a helicopter. If one day it is built, it would have a hybrid diesel-and-electric power unit. Flight would be assured by two stacked contra-rotating rotors, like a one-person version of the Russian Kamov-27. This system would be foldable for road use. At this juncture no more is known about the project, Boeing merely making vague declarations about the undoubted usefulness of PAVs in the future and about the company's interest in developing a model that is easy to use and – as ever – would cost the same as an up-market motor car. After this announcement, which was widely reported on in the media, Phantom Works, a Boeing R&D unit, refused to comment further on its work in this area, citing its 'purely conceptual' nature.

Just as speculative is the PALV of Spark Design of the Netherlands: a mixture of small autogyro and a closed motorcycle, the device is supposed to be capable of 120mph on the road and to be able to take off in only 50 yards. The concept is probably viable. Not only was it tested successfully by Harold Pitcairn in the 1930s (see Chapter 2) but it has recently been adapted for personal use.

At the beginning of 2005 Californian Sean Cooper built an autogyro from plans bought on the internet for $100 and based on the design of the Italian Magni Gyro. After having adapted it for road use, he obtained the authorisation of the Department of Motor Vehicles to use it on the road and in the air. His autogyro can only have the pilot on board and it has to stay in first gear, and it takes a good 20 minutes to remove the rotor and change to small-car mode. But Cooper seems to be on the right track: the machine only cost $30,000 and demanded only 20 hours of flying time for Cooper to get a pilot's licence. Above all, it can fly at 100mph over the clogged highways of Los Angeles....

Sean Cooper seems to be above all a clever hobbyist, which is hardly a portent of commercial success for his invention. That said, Larry R. Neal has managed to sell 20 or so of his similar Super Sky Cycle, so maybe times have changed. After all, this type of invention today fits perfectly into the framework of the conquest of airspace as imagined by American industry and government.

This is because the approach initiated by NASA in the area of door-to-door air transport is radically different from what was explored in the past. Far from wanting to create the all-purpose machine dear to Ted Hall and his like, this policy in effect separates personal flying vehicles according to their functions: economic and versatile small planes for mid-range flights and hybrids with limited on-road performance for urban and short-distance work.

It is not just a matter of the PAVs and their technological innovations being achievable at modest cost. It is their integration into a system that is really revolutionary. They are intended to be flown by pilots having only a basic level of knowledge, but with information systems to back them up; they will be capable of serving destinations with limited infrastructure; they will be complementary to existing means of transport. They are thus completely fresh vehicles, seen as occupying their own special niche and having a limited pattern of usage.

The PAVs represent a move towards a democratisation of airspace, making it accessible to the average American, or even the average European: the system could equally well operate on the Old Continent, there being 500 aerodromes in France alone and the same number in the United Kingdom.

So what is being promised us is nothing less than a new age of mobility. This will not bring with it the development of verticalist townscapes – we are a long way from what was imagined in *The Fifth Element*. On the contrary, just like the car and the road network in the 20th century, the Personal Airborne Vehicle and the 'Highways in the Sky' invite us to push our horizon ever further into the distance and – paradoxically, perhaps – mark a new stage in the extension of our territorial ambitions on dry land.

Optimists can dream of being able to live in the green of the countryside and work in the town centre. Others will doubtless have a vision of the multiplication of built-up areas, the creation of endless suburbs or meta-urbs, making our countries a little like a super-LA.

In his 1997 film *The Fifth Element*, Luc Besson brought flying cars front-stage again, with these vehicles conceived by Jean-Claude Mézières, father of comic-strip hero Valérian. Even if the film's sources of inspiration are numerous – from Enki Bilal's comic-strips to the film *Heavy Metal* – the car chase sequences, between taxis and police cars, are quite spectacular.

# Conclusion: Manifesto for a success with no future

*"The world is as we know it now to be, and always has been: everyone forgets that it could be, or ever was, other than the way it is now."*

*John Crowley,* Love and Sleep

### The end of the dream

The 21st century is well underway, and the world is still waiting for a viable flying car to be put on sale.

All the engineers who have worked on these hybrid vehicles have quickly understood one basic truth: the flying car might well bring together the advantages of the two different forms of transport, but it also unfortunately combines all their individual inconveniences. As a plane, the pilot has to contend with a device that is heavy, noisy, uncomfortable and cramped, whilst having a modest performance; as an automobile, the result risks being a pipsqueak micro-car of limited ability on the road.

To move on from such frankly mediocre dual-function machines, numerous technical problems need to be solved along the way, necessitating a substantial financial investment. One man working alone might succeed in building a machine, putting all his energy – and all his money – into the venture. But that can only ever be the first step. Afterwards the public and the business world have to be convinced, and the stumbling blocks are many: only a vehicle having production and sales structures behind it can hope to have a chance of being anything but a curiosity.

Compounding the problem, the flying car has always been tied to the aviation industry – which operates on the basis of limited production and high costs – rather than to the car industry, which is more attuned to making affordable everyday vehicles.

A further important factor came into play at the end of the Second World War, when at one stage it briefly looked as if the flying car might become a commercial reality. It was assumed that a new and sizeable market for private aircraft would come into being. In the end, however, people preferred using the big airlines and national car-hire networks. Further to this, the passion of Americans for their car didn't extent to planes. The arrival of the helicopter didn't help, as it annexed several niche markets such as the military and rescue and surveillance services.

Meanwhile some people had already solved the problem of their mobility without waiting for the flying car, a case in point being the people living in Casa de Aero, in Illinois. More than a village, this community was in fact a residential aerodrome, with its forty houses spread out one side or the other of a half-mile airstrip. The residents, for the most part employees of Chicago International Airport, went to work during the week in a private jet.

Certain basic practicalities also intruded. In the mind of the general public, private planes were expensive and complicated to use. Not only that, but before getting behind the wheel – or joystick – of an Aerocar or Airphibian, the driver/pilot would have had to obtain both a driving licence and a pilot's licence. Even then, his safety wouldn't have been assured, as there was nobody policing the airspace, and computer-assistance was in the future.

It was hardly surprising, therefore, that governments – in reality the US government, as the only one to have seriously considered the problem – had hesitated at the thought of a sky filled with thousands of machines operated by inexperienced pilots. Consequently certification in accordance with ever more stringent legislation made the legal aspect of these dual-function vehicles complicated, to say the least. Best not to think, either, about the costs of insuring such devices...

So is it an impossible dream, the flying car? Of course not: as we've seen, they have existed, they have flown, and they have even been made in small numbers.

It remains the case, though, that the only truly successful examples have been those linked to brilliant inventors of unparalleled tenacity, such as Waldo Waterman, Robert

Fulton, Ted Hall and Molt Taylor. Up until now, the history of the flying car has thus been above all a personal adventure.

Alongside the solitude of genius, the difficulty of the task has rendered the enterprise extremely fragile. The slightest incident – running out of fuel, the hesitancy or greed of investors, a delay in starting production – has been sufficient to kick the dream into touch. Above all, these visionaries were born too early. They tried to bring their ideas to life, even in a non-definitive form, at a time when society considered their machines to be nothing more than wacky suburban fantasies.

Perhaps things have changed: perhaps time has caught up and in the future the use of composite materials and computer technology will solve the last of the technical problems that confronted these pioneers. Other snags will come up, of course, such as the declining stock of fossil fuels. But a new generation of inventors is already trying to overcome this problem, such as Bert Rutan, who for his SpaceShipOne has specified an inert fuel based on Nitrous Oxide (laughing gas) and rubber .

Meanwhile, the projections of NASA are based on machines piloted by a professional, or entirely automated, and intended to operate away from towns rather than fly around them. These studies have looked at travel patterns as a whole, and give hybrid vehicles a real chance. But these are not flying cars in the strict sense of the word, but 'Personal Airborne Vehicles'. They will do everything for you and you won't have to worry about anything. You won't just be guided: you'll be overseen, and even directed.

This isn't the dream of absolute freedom to travel wherever one wants that Robert Fulton and Syd Mead envisaged. There is no way that the flying car as conceived by the engineers of the 1940s or by fantasy writers of various times will become a reality in today's world. It will remain a symbol of a future that was once promised to us, an emblem of science-fiction fantasy.

For the flying car is also an object of pure science-fiction, a device of personal liberation, destined for anyone and everyone and whose use is portrayed as profoundly transforming our society. It is only through a string of coincidences that it has strayed into the Real.

All things considered, and given the evolution of our societies and our way of life, to possess and use a machine such as the ConvAirCar has no great practical interest for most of us – decent public transport can probably provide everything we need. But the important thing is to continue to surprise oneself by dreaming of what one would do if one had such a flying car. Think of the gain in personal liberty that such a machine would bring to our life – in freeing us from traffic jams, in freeing us from being tied to timetables! Life would be so much better behind the wheel of an Aérauto than a Renault Twingo!

It's the power to imagine that we need – not necessarily to possess. Exemplary science-fiction object, artefact of a different future, key component of the Great Tomorrow, tool of liberation and grandeur, the flying car belongs to an alternative world.

To use it to transport ourselves from this side of the looking-glass to the other is a magnificent notion, providing – of course – that one doesn't actually succeed.

In Manhattan, the Downtown Skyport near Wall Street allows businessmen in a hurry to touch down in the heart of New York. The practice is still reserved for the elite, but in a glimpse into an imaginary near-future offered by this pre-war artwork it is suggested that aviation will become within the reach of everyone (*Life* magazine, 16 August 1937).

The Curtiss Bee, an experimental hover-car, was supposed to look like
this illustration and was intended to herald a new era in personal travel.
But this artwork was nothing more than a designer's wishful thinking.
The real Curtiss Bee, tested in 1959, was a hideous and dreadfully noisy
flying saucer that was incapable of rising more than an inch or two off
the ground. The project was soon abandoned.

# Chronology

1905   Death of Jules Verne

1906   Trajan Vuia flies his plane

1917   Glenn Curtiss shows Autoplane at Pan-American Aeronautic Exposition, New York

1918   First patent for flying car, lodged by Felix Longobardi

1921   René Tampier's Avion-automobile travels down Champs-Elysées

1933   Announcement of Eugene Vidal's competition to design a low-priced aircraft

1936   Pitcairn AC-35 autogyro demonstrated to US administration

1937   First flight of Waldo Waterman's Arrowbile

1939   Theodore P. Hall begins tests of his Roadable Airplane

1943   Raoul Hafner's Rotabuggy tested

1944   First tests of Convair 103 of William B. Stout and George G. Spratt

1946   Ted Hall flies the Hall Flying Car, the Southern Aircraft Corporation Aerocar, and the Convair 116

1946   First flight of Robert Fulton's Airphibian

1947   The ConvAirCar makes debut in skies over San Diego

1949   Test flight of modified version of James Wisner Holland's Ercoupe

1949   First official flight of Molt Taylor's Aerocar

1950   Presentation across Italy of Luigi Pellarini's Aerauto

1950   Robert Fulton's Airphibian FA-2 is first flying car to obtain certification from US administration

1952   Homologation of Airphibian FA-3

1956   First flight of Lewis Jackson's Versatile 1

1956   Homologation of Aerocar

1957   First flight of Waldo Waterman's Aerobile

1957   Bruce Hallock's Road Wing tested

1959   First flight of Joseph Halsmer's Aircar

1959   Herbert Trautman has the fright of his life at controls of Road Air

1961   Walt Disney film *The Absent-Minded Professor*

1968   *Chitty Chitty Bang Bang* film

1968   Molt Taylor's Aerocar III takes to the air

1973   Henry Smolinski and Harold Blake die in AVE Mizar

1974   Leland Bryan dies on board his Model 111

1976   Robert Lebouder flies from Paris to Biarritz in his Autoplane

1978   Fire at San Diego Aerospace Museum and destruction of Ted Hall's Roadable Airplane

1982   Ridley Scott film *Blade Runner*

1983   K.P. Price begins testing Volante I

1989   First tests of Paul Moller's M200X

1997   Luc Besson film *The Fifth Element*

1998   Tests of CarterCopter begin

2000   Roland Magallon unveils ultra-light flying car

2003   Tests of K.P. Rice's Volante II

2004   Press launch for Boeing's Personal Air Vehicle

2005   Enki Bilal film *Ad Vitam*

2005   Demonstration of 'Small Aircraft Transportation System' (SATS)

2009   Death in Jetpod of Michael Dacre, head of Avcen Ltd

2009   Successful tests of Terrafugia's Transition

# Bibliography

## General

*Jane's All the World's Aircraft*, published annually since 1909
*ConvAirCar 1948*, sales catologue, Convair, 1948
*En direct du futur*, Paris, Casterman, 1979 (1974), pp. 55-57
et 117-122
Jacques Borgé et Nicolas Viasnoff, *Les véhicules hors série en 300 histoires et 150 photos*, Paris, Balland, 1976, pp. 180-185
Ron Borovec, *Roadable Aircraft Magazine*, 14 issues since July 1992
Peter Bowers, *Curtiss Airplanes since 1907*, London, Putnam, 1979, p. 75
Courtland Canby, *Histoire de l'aéronautique*, Lausanne, Rencontre, 1962, p. 11
Bruce H. Charnov, *From Autogiro to Gyroplane: The Amazing Survival of an Aviation Technology*, Westport, Praeger Publishers, 2003
George W. Green, "Flying Cars, Amphibious Vehicles and Other Dual Mode Transports", Jefferson, McFarland, 2010
A. Guichard, *L'année scientifique*, Lausanne, Edita, 1958
Louis Pauwels (dir.), *Encylopédie Planète: Profil du futur*, Paris, Denoël, 1964, pp. 59-73.
Jake Schultz, "A Drive in the Clouds, The Story of the Aerocar", New Brighton, Flying Books, 2006
Palmer Stiles, *Roadable Aircraft, from Wheels to Wings*, Melbourne (FL), Palmer Stiles Ed., 1994
John Wegg, *General Dynamics Aircraft and their Predecessors*, London, Putnam, 1990, pp. 184-186
Bill Yenne, *The World's Worst Aircraft*, New York, Barnes & Noble Books, 1999 (1987)

## Science fiction

Brian Aldiss, David Wingrove, *Trillion Year Spree*, New York, Doubleday, 1986
Brian Ash (ed.), *The Visual Encyclopedia of Science Fiction*, London, Triune Books, 1978
Yves Aumont, Thierry Saurat, *Cinémas de science-fiction*, Nantes, L'Atalante, 1985

Neil Barron, *Anatomy of Wonder: a Critical Guide to Science Fiction*, New York, Bowker, 1987
Lucian Boia, *Pour une histoire de l'imaginaire*, Paris, Les Belles Lettres, 1998
John Clute, Peter Nicholls (ed.), *The Encyclopedia of Science Fiction*, New York, St. Martin's Griffin, 1993
Roger Fulton, *The Encyclopedia of TV Science Fiction*, London, Boxtree, 1995
Ronald Hahn, Volker Jansen, *Das Heyne Lexikon des Science Fiction Films*, München, Heyne, 1993
David G. Hartwell, *Age of Wonders*, New York, Tor, 1996
Edward James, *Science Fiction in the Twentieth Century*, Oxford, Oxford University Press, 1994
Gilbert Millet et Denis Labbé, *La Science-fiction*, Paris, Belin, coll. Sujets, 2002
Lorris Murail, *La Science-fiction*, Paris, Larousse, 1999
David Pringle, *The Ultimate Guide to Science Fiction*, London, Grafton, 1990
Jaques Sadoul, *Histoire de la science-fiction moderne*, Paris, Laffont, 1984
Darko Suvin, *Metamorphoses of Science Fiction: On the Poetics and History of a Literary Genre*. New Haven, Yale University Press, 1979
Pierre Versins, *Encyclopédie de l'Utopie, des voyages extraordinaires et de la science fiction*, Lausanne, L'Âge d'Homme, 1972
Donald Wollheim, *Les faiseurs d'univers*, Paris, Laffont, 1972

## Bibliography

Pierre Versins, *Les moyens de transport individuels dans les littératures conjecturales romanesques rationnalisées, une chrono-bibliographie thématique*, Lausanne, Club Futopia, 1964

## Articles

*L'Aérophile*, 1-15 December, 1921, Paris, p. 362
*L'Aéronautique*, 1921, p. 493
*Mechanix Illustrated*, November 1955, pp. 109-111
*Science et Vie*, n° 353, February 1947, p. 55 ff.
*Superboy*, n° 5, February 1950, p. 59

"A Car that Flies is a Plane that Drives", in *Parade*, 25 January 1948, pp. 22-23

"Aerocar Dream Still Flying", in *Popular Mechanics*, August 1988, p. 16

"Air Inventions", in *Life*, 25 October 1948, pp. 139-144.

"Close-up of ConvairCar", in *Aviation Week*, 19 April 1948, p. 21

"The Flying Auto", in *Mechanics and Handicraft*, vol. 4, n° 12, January 1938, p. 47

"Flying Cars are Here", in *Motor Trend*, December 1951, vol. 3, n° 12, pp. 16-17

"Flying Cars Swoop to the Rescue", on *BBC News online*, 22 September 2004

"Flying Taxi Vision for Commuters", on *BBC News online*, 7 November 2004

"Fulgur, la voiture de rêve", in *Les Echos Simca*, n° 87, Paris, October 1958, pp. 18-20

"Home-Made Roadable Readied by L.A. Inventors", in *Aviation*, February 1947, pp. 64-65

"I Fly My Automobile", in *Air Facts*, 1 July 1950, pp. 11-27

"La jeep volante est née", in *Science et Vie*, n° 488, May 1958, pp. 108-110

"La maison rationnelle en l'an 2000", in *Meccano magazine*, n° 7, May 1958, pp. 14-15

"Paris-Londres en voitures volantes", in *Meccano magazine*, n° 3, January 1958, pp. 24-25

"Personal Aircraft Development – An Official Report", in *Aero Digest*, vol. 59, n° 6, December 1949, pp. 19-23 et 87-88

"Plane-Auto", in *Mechanix Illustrated*, October 1946, pp. 67 et 165

"Private Flying", in *The Aeroplane*, 28 November 1947, p. 715

"Robert E. Fulton Jr., Globetrotting Inventor of the Airphibian, the Gunairstructor and the Skyhook (obituary)", in *The Times*, May 15, 2004

"Robert Fulton and his Airphibian", in *FAA General Aviation News*, March 1978, pp. 11-13

"Rocatomic", in *Sciences et techniques pour tous*, n° 14, December 1947, p. 28

"The SAC Aerocar", in *Air Classics*, September 1986, pp. 68-71

"Southern Aircraft tests the Roadable, Combination Automobile and Airplane", in *Western Flying*, March 1946, p. 66

"The Spratt-Stout Flying Automobile", in *Popular Mechanics*, June 1945

"Teacher Builds Roadable Plane", in *Aviation Week*, 17 December 1956, p. 113

"La vie en l'an 2000", in *Science et Vie*, n° 500, May 1959, pp. 36 et ss.

"La voiture de demain", in *Science-Fiction magazine*, n° 1, 1953, p. 12

"Waterman Arrowbile", in *Historical Aviation Album* (Collector's Series), n° 3, 1966, pp. 132-138

"Where's my Flying Car?", in *NASA Explores*, 1 February, 2001

Edmond Blanc, "Le mariage de l'avion et de l'automobile", in *Sciences et voyages*, n° 18, May 1947, pp. 150-152

Victor Boesen, "Fly It or Drive It", in *Flying Sportsman and Skyways*, September 1947, pp. 54-59

David A. Brown, "Firm Designs Aircraft that Drives like Car", in *Aviation Week & Space Technology*, 1 November 1993, pp. 67-69

Dennis M. Bushnell, "Advanced Civilian Aeronautical Concepts", NASA Langley Research Center, 1996

James R. Chiles, "Flying Cars were a Dream that Never Got off the Ground", in *Smithsonian*, vol. 19, n° 11, February 1989, pp. 144-159

Leighton Collins, "The Airphibian", in *Air Facts*, 1 January 1947, pp. 9-21

Leighton Collins, "Fulton's Airphibian", *Air Facts*, 1 July 1947, pp. 52-74

Joseph J. Corn, "An Airplane in Every Garage", in *Regency*, 1981, pp. 62-69

Jack Cox, "Aerocar: Molt Taylor's Quest for a more Useful Airplane", in *Sport Aviation*, January 1990, pp. 11-21

Steven C. Crow, "A Practical Flying Car", SAE International/AIAA, 1997

Alexis Dawydoff, "The Roadable Airplane: Certainty or Absurdity?", in *Air Trails*, August 1949, pp. 21 et ss.

Luc Debraine, "L'étrange voiture volante du Dr Paul Moller", in *Le Temps*, 9 March 2001, p. 48

Luc Debraine, "Le Jetpod, taxi du ciel", in *Le Temps*, 8 March 2005, p. 36

Luc Debraine, "La voiture volante redécolle", in *Le Temps*, 19 November 2004, p. 34

Michael Fessier Jr., "The Flying Car and the Men Who Believe", in *LA Weekly*, 16-22 January, 1998, pp. 25-32

Zsolt Eugenio Geza Follmann et Adilson Marques da Cunha, "Triphibian Flying Car Design", SAE International/AIAA, 1997

Duncan Forgan, "Flying Cars nearly ready for Take-off", in *The Scotsman*, 31 August 2004

Gregory Freiherr, "What has Four Wheels and Flies? The Dream of a Roadable Airplane Continues", in *Smithsonian Air & Space Magazine*, December 1995/January 1996

Benjamin Fulford et Patricia Huang, "Honda Takes to the Skies", in *Forbes Magazine online*, 15 November 2004

Jonathan Glancey, "Taking to the Skies", in *In.Tech*, 28 June 2005, pp. 19-20

John Grossman, "Auto Pilots, Air and Space", in *Smithsonian*, vol. 10, n°5, December 1995 - January 1996

Lew Holt, "Flying Tanks Shed Their Wings", in *Modern Mechanics and Inventions*, July 1932, pp. 34-37

Nonie Horton, "At Last a Roadable Ercoupe", in *Air Facts*, 1 February 1949, pp. 28-29

Karlheinz Kens, "Kommt ein Auto geflogen", in *Hobby, Das Magazin der Technik*, August 1956, pp. 9-15

Olga Kharif, "A Flying Leap for Cars", sur *BusinessWeek online*, 25 August 2004

Brendan I. Koerner, "Have You Flown a Ford Lately?", on *Slate.msn.com*, 25 June 2003

G. Labadié-Lagrave, "La civilisation en 2200", in *Lecture du dimanche*, free supplement to *Feuille d'avis de Lausanne*, Vol. VII, 1897, p. 215

Robert C. Lunch, "Waterman's New Flying Wing", in *Popular Aviation*, November 1935, pp. 287-88 et 336

Tarik Malik, "NASA Sets Stage for Personal Aircraft", on *Space.com*, 18 August 2004

Matt Marshall, "Commuting to Silicon Valley... by Gyroplane", in *The Mercury News*, June 10, 2005

Mark D. Moore, "Personal Air Vehicles: A Rural/Regional and Intra-urban On-demand Transportation System", American Institute of Aeronautics and Astronautics, 2003

Alexander McSurely, "Two New Roadable Planes Renew Attack on Old Problem", in *Aviation News*, 18 November 1946, pp. 15-16

Xavier Meal, "American Fly-Drive: The Taylor Aerocar", in *Aeroplane Monthly*, vol. 27, n° 1, January 1999

R. G. Naugle, "Practical Design Considerations for... A Retractable Roadable Airplane", in *Western Flying*, February 1949, pp. 16-17

Wolfgang Ott, "HELIos, a VTOL Flying Car", SAE International/AIAA, 1998

Jerry Phillips, "The Waterman Arrowbile", in *Aviation Quarterly*, vol. 5, n° 1, First Quarter 1979

Wesley Price, "The Automobile Gets Wings", in *The Saturday Evening Post*, May 17, 1947, pp. 28-29 et 51-55

Aude Raux, "Retour raté vers le futur", in *VSD*, 23 January 2003, pp. 56-57

Ben Robin, "Fulton Airphibian", in *Flying*, August 1950, pp. 24-25 et 58-60

Gary Sanders, "Boeing Technical Experts Check the Feasibility of Personal Air Vehicles", on *Boeing Frontiers online*, Vol. 3, Issue 3, July 2004

Gordon Smith, "From the Curb to the Clouds: a Brief History of the Flying Car", in *Popular Mechanics*, 7 October 1982, pp. 26-29

George G. Spratt, "The Controlwing Aircraft", in *Sport Aviation*, June 1974, p. 48 ff and July 1974, p. 25 ff

Thomas E. Stimson Jr., "Your Aerial Sedan for 1967", in *Popular Mechanics Magazine*, July 1957, pp. 74-78

Palmer C. Stiles, "History and Future of Flying Automobiles", SAE International/AIAA, 23 June 1992

William B. Stout, "Can We Have a Universal Vehicle?", in *Flying Magazine*, June 1948, p. 31 ff

Frank A. Tinker, "I Flew It", in *Popular Mechanics*, August 1971, p. 89 ff

Pat Tobin, "It Flies! It Drives! It's the Aerocar!", in *Special Interest Autos*, n° 141, May/June 1994, pp. 50-57 and 70

Walt Woron, "Of Wings and Wheels: an Investigation of the Flying Car", in *Automobile Quarterly*, vol. 22, n° 1, 1984, p. 95 ff.

Charline Zeitoun/David Pouilloux, "Et vole la bagnole!", in *Science et Vie Junior*, n° 120, September 1999, pp. 26-28

**Internet sites**

**General sites**

www.aerofiles.com – Aerofiles: A Century of American Aviation
www.aerospacemuseum.org – San Diego Aerospace Museum
www.ailleurs.ch – Maison d'Ailleurs, Musée de la science-fiction

The Triphibion: for land, sea and air, as proclaimed on the cover of the March 1936 edition of *Mechanics and Handicraft*. The prototype caught fire during the first attempt to get it working, and the project stopped there.

*Cohen works for Barris-Watford, who publish big, trendy "trade" paperbacks: illustrated histories of the neon sign, the pinball machine, the windup toys of Occupied Japan. (...) Cohen introduced us and explained that Dialta was the prime mover behind the latest Barris-Watford project, an illustrated history of what she called "American Streamlined Moderne." Cohen called it "raygun Gothic." Their working title was* The Airstream Futuropolis: The Tomorrow That Never Was.

*(...) I found myself remembering Sunday morning television in the Fifties. Sometimes they'd run old eroded newsreels as filler on the local station. You'd sit there with a peanut butter sandwich and a glass of milk, and a static-ridden Hollywood baritone would tell you that there was* A Flying Car in Your Future. *And three Detroit engineers would putter around with this big old Nash with wings, and you'd see it rumbling furiously down some deserted Michigan runway.*

William Gibson, "The Gernsback Continuum"

www.airspacemag.com – Air & Space Smithsonian Magazine
www.eaa.org – Experimental Aircraft Association
www.museumofflight.org – Seattle Museum of Flight
www.nasm.si.edu – Smithsonian National Air and Space Museum

**Specialist sites**

www.aerocar.com – Sweeney Aerocar
www.afaco.com – Advanced Flying Automobile Sokol 400
www.cartercopters.com – Carter Aviation Technologies
www.dual-use.com – Aeromaster Synergy
www.gizio.it – Cellcraft
www.haynes-aero.com – Haynes Skyblazer
www.hiller.org – Hiller Aviation Museum
www.labicheaerospace.com – LaBiche Aerospace FSC-1
www.macroindustries.com – Macro SkyRider
www.moller.com – Moller Skycar Volantor
www.roadabletimes.com – The Roadable Times Flying Car Register
www.skywalkervtol.com – Mirror Image Aerospace Skywalker
www.strongware.com/dragon – Magic Dragon Aircar
www.taero.com – Aerospectives tAero 4000
www.transairsystems.com – Trans Air Systems Flying Motorcycle
www.trekaero.com – Trek Aerospace Springtail
www.urbanaero.com – X-Hawk Aerial Vehicle
www.volanteaircraft.com – Volante Aircraft Flying Car

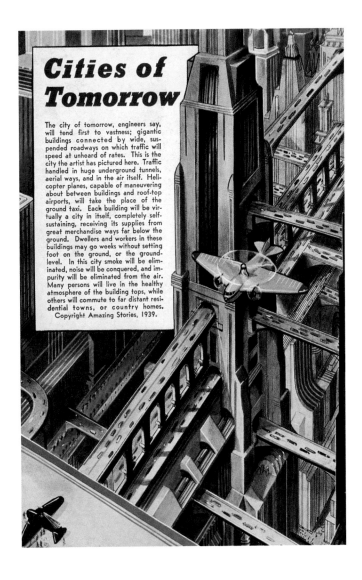

**Cities of Tomorrow**

The city of tomorrow, engineers say, will tend first to vastness; gigantic buildings connected by wide, suspended roadways on which traffic will speed at unheard of rates. This is the city the artist has pictured here. Traffic handled in huge underground tunnels, aerial ways, and in the air itself. Helicopter planes, capable of maneuvering about between buildings and roof-top airports, will take the place of the ground taxi. Each building will be virtually a city in itself, completely self-sustaining, receiving its supplies from great merchandise ways far below the ground. Dwellers and workers in these buildings may go weeks without setting foot on the ground, or the ground-level. In this city smoke will be eliminated, noise will be conquered, and impurity will be eliminated from the air. Many persons will live in the healthy atmosphere of the building tops, while others will commute to far distant residential towns, or country homes. Copyright Amazing Stories, 1939.

'Cities of Tomorrow' in an illustration by Julian S. Krupa for the August 1939 (vol.13 no.8) issue of *Amazing Stories*. 'In 50 years, this city will be a reality,' predicted the magazine.

**Acknowledgements**

I would like to thank the following for their support in the course of writing and researching this book:

Pierre-Marcel Favre | Yves Bosson (Agence Martienne) | Francis Valéry

Maison d'Ailleurs: Emmanuel Barraud, Jennifer Bochud, Philippe Ney, Patricia Pacheco, Richard Tanniger, Jean Terrier | San Diego Aerospace Museum: Alan Renga, Casey Smith | Smithonian National Air and Space Museum (Washington, DC): Allan Janus, Kristine L. Kaske | Carter Aviation Technologies: Rod Anderson, Claudius Klimt, Mat Recardo | Lost Highways Archives: Todd B. Kimmell, Jared Rosenbaum | Macro Industries: David Atchison, Marcia Elkins, Norris Luce | Marsu Productions: Valérie David-Gooris, Dominique Paquet, Céline Rannou | Trans Air Systems: Fran Macalino, Tom McNally | Vectis Ltd.: Stuart Basinger, Lorna Kaufman | at-elier: Julien Notter, Sébastien Vigne

Cuno Affolter (Bibliothèque municipale de Lausanne) | Alain Bielik | Bruce H. Charnov | André Chevailler (Cinémathèque suisse de Lausanne) | Marcus Conder | Stephen P. Cook (Ford Motor Company) | Kent Crookston (Mirror Images Aerospace) | Nick D'Acquisto | Ken Dayer (Jay Miller Aviation History Collection) | Larry Dwyer (Aviation History Online Museum) | Larry Elie | Harry Einstein | Harry W. Falk | Chip Fyn | Jean-Noël Gex (Ilford) | Cindy Guignard | Jean-David Gyger | Robin Haynes | Paul Hernandez (Harmer E. Davis Transportation Library) | Bill Higgins | Gino d'Ignazio Leslie Kendall (Petersen Automotive Museum) | Mitchell LaBiche | Mael Le Mée | Susan A. Lurvey (EAA Library) | Tucker Madawick | Jean-Michel Margot | Claudia Meyer (Avcen Ltd.) | Jennifer Moller | Mark D. Moore (NASA Langley) | Sally Jane Norman | Robert Pegg (Performance Aviation Manufacturing) | Stephen Pitcairn | James Powers | Ken Quimby (Arkansas Aviation Historical Society)| Les Retraires Populaires | K. P. Rice | David Saunders | Simon Scott (Kestrel Ltd.) | Walt P. Shiel | Jeff Spitzer (Synergy) | Palmer Stiles | Johan Visschedijk | Hampton Wayt | Katherine Williams (Museum of Flight, Seattle)

As well as
Ariane Turini | Gilles Goy
and
Honor Harger

**Picture credits**

Coll. Maison d'Ailleurs/Agence Martienne: pp. 7, 11, 13 a, 13 b, 17 a-b, 18, 19, 20 a-b, 21 c, 36, 47 a, 48, 49 b, 51 a-b, 55 a-b, 56, 59 a, 59 c, 60, 61 a-b, 62 a-b, 63 a, 69 b, 77 b, 78 a-b, 79 b, 83 a-b, 88, 89 a-b, 97 a, 100, 103, 104 a-c, 105 a, 116 a-b, 117, 118 a-b, 119, 123 a, 128 a, 128 c, 130 b, 133, 137 a, 140, 145 a, 147 a, 148 b, 149, 152 b, 155 a-c, 171 a, 183 | coll. Maison d'Ailleurs: pp. 12, 31, 47 b, 59 b, 63 b, 93 b, 94, 95 b-c, 96, 97 b, 99, 101, 105 b, 128 b, 129, 136, 139 b, 144 a, 147 b, 151 b, 154, 169 b, 171 b, 191 a| coll. Agence Martienne: pp. 16, 21 a-b, 191 b | Smithonian National Air and Space Museum (Washington, DC): pp. 8, 14, 22, 23, 24, 37, 38, 40, 80, 84, 86, 87, 108, 112, 113, 114, 115 | Smithonian National Air and Space Museum/ Associated Press: p. 32 | San Diego Aerospace Museum: pp. 28, 34, 44, 52, 53, 66, 70-71, 72, 73 a, 74, 75, 76, 77 a | coll. Hampton Wayt: pp. 50 a-b, 64 b, 65, 73 b, 79 a, 106 a-b, 107 a-c, 134 a-b, 135 a-c, 169 a, 178 a | United States Patent and Trademark Office: pp. 15 b, 26, 43 b-c, 49 a, 54 a-b, 93 a, 98, 130 a, 131 a-c | Cinémathèque suisse de Lausanne: pp. 64 a, 90, 124, 132 a-b, 159 a-b, 161 | The Wright Brothers Aeroplane Company (Dayton, Ohio): p. 15 a | Johan Visschedijk/1000aircraftphotos.com: p. 27 | Todd B. Kimmell/Lost Highways Archive & Research Library: p. 41 | Pitcairn Aircraft Archives/Stephen Pitcairn: p. 42 a-c | Bibliothèque municipale de Lausanne: p. 95 a | Jay Miller Aviation History Collection: p. 102 a-d | Alamy Images: p. 69 a | zéro50 – fond d'art-chives: pp. 25, 43 a | Museum of Flight, Seattle: pp. 111, 122, 123 b | www.fiddlersgreen.net/Chip Fyn: p. 120 | Salon Rétromobile/Robert Lebouder: p. 127 a-c | K. P. Rice: p. 138 a-c | Scaled Composites LLC: p. 137 b | Vectis Auctions Ltd. (www.vectis.co.uk): p. 139 a | Ford Motor Company: pp. 144 b, 163 | Marsu Productions (www.marsuproductions.com): p. 145 b | Moller International Inc.: pp. 142, 143 a-b, 146, 148 a | Macro Industries: pp. 150, 151 a | Kestrel Aerospace Ltd.: p. 153 | Trek Aerospace: p. 152 a | Allied Aerotechnics: p. 153 c | Mirror Images Aerospace: p. 153 b | Gino d'Ignazio (www.gizio.it): p. 153 d-e | Gino d'Ignazio/PAM: p. 153 f-g | LaBiche Aerospace: p. 159 c | Aeromaster Innovations: p. 159 d | Haynes Aero: p. 160 a | Trans Air Systems: p. 160 b | Walter P. Shiel: pp. 156, 162 | coll. Alain Bielik: pp. 181 | National Aeronautics and Space Administration (NASA): pp. 172, 173 a-b, 177 a-b, 178 b, 179 b | Avcen Ltd.: pp. 173 c-d | Carter Aviation Technologies: pp. 166, 174, 175 | Keystone/AP Photo/John Froschauer: p. 179 a | Magni Gyro: p. 180 a | Spark Design: p. 180 b | Harmer E. Davis Transportation Library: p. 186 | Front cover: San Diego Aerospace Museum – ConvAirCar 118 of Theodore P. Hall | Rear cover: San Diego Aerospace Museum, Lost Highways Archive & Research Library, Moller International Inc.

*For pages with several illustrations, the 'a' and 'b' etc. identifications refer first to the left-hand column, from top to bottom, and then to the right-hand column, again from top to bottom.*